A MEDIUM TERM STRATEGY
FOR EMPLOYMENT
AND MANPOWER POLICIES

ORGANISATION FOR ECONOMIC CO-OPERATION AND DEVELOPMENT

The Organisation for Economic Co-operation and Development (OECD) was set up under a Convention signed in Paris on 14th December 1960, which provides that the OECD shall promote policies designed:
— to achieve the highest sustainable economic growth and employment and a rising standard of living in Member countries, while maintaining financial stability, and thus to contribute to the development of the world economy;
— to contribute to sound economic expansion in Member as well as non-member countries in the process of economic development;
— to contribute to the expansion of world trade on a multilateral, non-discriminatory basis in accordance with international obligations.
The Members of OECD are Australia, Austria, Belgium, Canada, Denmark, Finland, France, the Federal Republic of Germany, Greece, Iceland, Ireland, Italy, Japan, Luxembourg, the Netherlands, New Zealand, Norway, Portugal, Spain, Sweden, Switzerland, Turkey, the United Kingdom and the United States.

*
* *

Queries concerning permissions or translation rights should be addressed to:
Director of Information, OECD
2, rue André-Pascal, 75775 PARIS CEDEX 16, France.

TABLE OF CONTENTS

PREFACE

With the increasing likelihood that industrialised economies, and in particular labour markets, will continue to face growing structural imbalances, OECD Member countries are increasingly led to formulate their short-term economic and labour-market policies with a medium-term perspective in view. The OECD Manpower and Social Affairs Committee has therefore requested the Secretariat to prepare a report on medium-term labour market development, in order to clarify the proper role of selective employment and manpower policies within a medium-term strategy aimed at regaining full employment. The present report, which is published under the responsibility of the Secretary-General, has been written in response to the Manpower and Social Affairs Committee's request. It also incorporates some recent Secretariat work on unemployment carried out for the Economic Policy Committee's Working Party 2.

INTRODUCTION

THE SCOPE AND NATURE OF THE PROBLEM

THE CURRENT UNEMPLOYMENT SITUATION
AND THE MEDIUM-TERM OUTLOOK

For about three years, the rate of unemployment in the OECD area has hovered around 5 to 5½ per cent. In spite of a certain revival of demand and output since the middle of 1975 and a slight improvement in employment growth, the number of those out of work has remained at the high plateau reached in the middle of the recession (see Chart 1). Recorded unemployment is but one manifestation of the underutilisation of labour. Others include reductions in working hours, backflow of foreign workers, discouraged workers leaving the labour force, deteriorating human resources resulting from unused skills and a slowing down of productivity growth. If all these factors were taken into account, actual labour-market slack would seem to be much more severe than is indicated by recorded unemployment.

The persistent weakness of the current employment situation and the actual amount of labour-market slack suggest that a deeper appreciation of the situation requires a broader look, both in terms of analysis of past and probable future medium-term trends. If Diagrams 1-3 of Annex I are considered, it appears that since about 1969, a year in which unemployment increased in the OECD area as a whole, the trend in unemployment has been upwards irrespective of cyclical variations in economic activity. Diagram 1A shows that both the total labour force and employment (for the OECD area) rose steadily from 1965 onwards, with employment then decreasing in absolute terms after 1974. The total labour force has risen remarkably steadily, but total employment exhibits small spurts in the boom years of 1966, 1969 and 1973. But it is interesting to note that even with steady labour-force growth between 1965 and 1969, the total unemployment shown in Diagram 1B remained relatively constant at around six million people. Diagram 2 compares various countries' unemployment rates adjusted to United States standards, and this shows that in Canada, France and the United Kingdom the trend to higher unemployment may have begun as early as 1966. Finally, Diagram 3 shows the year-to-year percentage increases in unemployment rates. Since 1968, virtually every country (Austria, Greece, Norway and Sweden are exceptions) have experienced a majority of upward year-to-year changes in the unemployment level.

Of longer-run concern than the currently high levels of unemployment, which will recede with renewed economic growth, is the distinct possibility that the nature of unemployment is changing. If this is the case, one consequence is that unemployment may be less responsive to traditional demand-management policies. This conclusion is prompted by the rising trend in unemployment, and it is further substantiated by comparing unemployment rates at cyclical peaks, and job vacancies relative to rates of unemployment (see Chapter I).

What are the future prospects? As Diagram 1A illustrates, the present high levels of unemployment result to a large extent from the slowdown in economic

Chart 1

CIVILIAN LABOUR FORCE, CIVILIAN EMPLOYMENT
AND UNEMPLOYMENT, IN 11 OECD COUNTRIES[1]
(Seasonally adjusted)

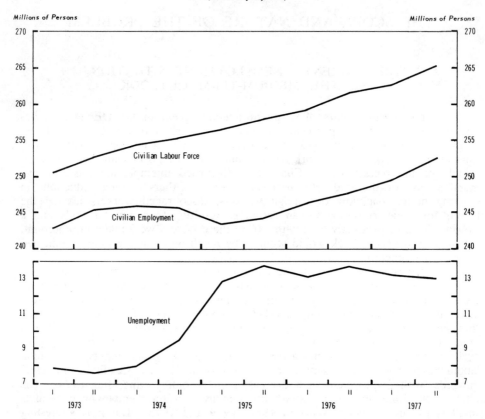

1. Canada, United States, Japan, Australia, Austria, Finland, Germany, Italy, Norway, Sweden, United Kingdom.
Source : OECD Labour Force Statistics.

growth, and will pick up in the medium-term. Hence, some portion of current unemployment will be responsive to general reflationary measures. However, projections of labour demand and supply (see Chapter I) suggest continuing high levels of unemployment over the medium term. Moreover, a number of structural changes in the nature of labour demand and supply, as well as changes in the functioning of labour markets, strengthen the trend to continuing high levels of unemployment.

THE IMPLICATIONS

It is important that adequate consideration be given to the economic and social costs of prolonged and large-scale unemployment. Involuntary unemployment implies a loss of potential output and a consequent relative decline in social welfare. It is a waste of human resources and a source of severe social and economic hardship. Rates of growth in per capita income have already shown significant deterioration in recent years in nearly all Member countries. Social transfer programmes (unemployment insurance, income transfers, etc.) have been claiming steadily-increasing shares of Member-country public sector budgets and thus have put constraints on the financial resources available for other areas of policy or have increased public sector borrowing requirements. Furthermore, the longer these high-unemployment rates persist, the less responsive is the problem to corrective policy efforts—human capital deteriorates, workers become discouraged and then permanently drop out of the labour market. For many of those above 45 years of age, the unemployment situation is often irreversible.

Large numbers of young people are reaching maturity without having had a meaningful employment experience. The consequences of this situation are serious. In economic terms it represents a missed opportunity for investing in human capital. Youths who are denied a meaningful work experience will reach labour-force maturity without having invested in a skill and work experience that, in turn, would generate a secure, lifetime flow of earnings. This situation can also have consequences of a social nature, or of a demoralising nature, on those trying to enter the labour force for the first time, or trying to re-enter. This is distinct from the potential human capital-investment loss measured in strictly economic terms. Poor access to the labour force for new entrants is different from the problem facing the disadvantaged who, because of chronic low productivity, are unable to secure steady, gainful employment and continue to encounter unemployment problems even under traditionally-defined conditions of full employment. Again, even though such people are usually the recipients of social support through income-transfer programmes, their continuing exclusion from meaningful employment is a problem that can have serious social consequences unless productive uses for their time can be found.

The analysis presented in Chapter I indicates that more than any other characteristic—sex, race, region, occupation or industry—it is *age* that currently most segments the labour force in terms of access to continuing employment opportunities. When enterprises treat labour as a fixed or quasi-fixed cost (and it is suggested later why this is increasingly the case), and the economy fails for a time to generate sufficient employment, a cleavage develops between those fortunate enough to secure jobs and continue in them, and those not so fortunate. Those in employment understandably enough create barriers and protective measures that will consolidate their positions, often by raising the hiring and dismissal costs to the employer.

Another implication of continuously high unemployment is its discouraging effect on the behaviour of the peripheral labour force—minorities, migrants, second family workers, youth, the involuntarily retired. These workers enter and leave the active labour force as economic opportunities rise and fall. But it would be an oversimplification to assume that this unstable employment behaviour results from affluence and that a prolonged denial of labour market access to those groups should not give rise to particular concern. Simply because these workers have left the labour force does not necessarily mean that they have done so willingly and their discouragement in finding a new job may be associated with considerable economic and social hardship.

Finally, there are also serious international implications of high and prolonged unemployment. The longer unemployment remains above levels which prevail during reasonably full utilisation of capacity, the greater are domestic demands for protectionism. Trade restrictions obviously have grave implications for the trading structure of OECD countries. Furthermore, the problem is particularly acute for developing Member countries which have neither the natural resources nor the manufactured goods with which to purchase them. Along with general problems of high consumption and capital goods costs, these countries share the burden of depressed international demand for labour inequitably. Adding to their difficulties has been the decision taken by a number of industrialised Member countries to restrict further inflows of foreign labour and to reduce existing levels by stimulating a return to their countries of origin.

THE CAUSES

Along with a variety of possible contributory forces which vary in importance from one country to another, there are three primary interacting causes both for the current situation and for assuming pessimistic employment prospects for some time to come: demand deficiency stemming mainly from constraints on demand-management policies and private uncertainty about the future; significant changes in the level and composition of labour supply, not accompanied by corresponding changes in the demand for labour; and constraints on other factor inputs (investment, energy) or changes in the cost and fixed nature of labour relative to these other inputs. Chapter II identifies two additional—albeit less significant—causes: labour-market shifts to the tertiary sector that have increased inflationary pressures which, in turn, have partially induced policy makers to run a tighter economy; and longer gross labour flows at every level of aggregate supply and demand, thus increasing the likelihood of a transitional type of unemployment.

Obviously a most important and pervasive influence is deficient demand. Unless goods and services can be sold, factors of production will not be hired, at least not in the private market. It is also important to bear in mind that the present deficiency of demand may not just be a cyclical phenomenon, but may stretch over several years, given present efforts to wind down the price-wage spiral and the danger of a resurgence of inflation.

Causes of unemployment other than demand deficiency have traditionally been labelled frictional and structural factors. But these distinctions have become increasingly blurred, particularly the term "structural unemployment" which has become a model of imprecision. When the term first became common in the early 1960's it was fairly narrowly defined. It was applied to the fact that the level, location or distribution of job characteristics demanded by employers differed from the level, location or distribution of job characteristics offered by the labour force, even in cases where the simple number of job vacancies was at least as great as the number of job seekers, i.e. when there was no demand-deficient unemployment. Corollary terms referred to "mismatches" between supply and demand or supply "bottlenecks". In more recent years the term "structural" has been broadened considerably to incorporate *any* changes in labour demand and supply which could lead to rises in unemployment at any given level of demand for goods and services. Thus, the coming to age of the post-war "baby boom", increases in female participation rates, rising unemployment benefits, or insufficient growth of capital stock relative to available labour

10

resources would, under the broader definition, be included as structural changes which lead to increases in structural unemployment[1].

It still remains extremely difficult to make a sharp empirical distinction between the effects of demand deficiency and structure. The longer demand deficiency continues, the more intransigent the unemployment problem becomes and thus the larger the structural component. This has particularly been the case during the present slow recovery, which has seen a marked tendency for structural rigidities in labour markets to increase. The lack of confidence in future demand prospects is inhibiting investment, thus raising the risk that future capital shortages and bottlenecks will appear before unemployed labour can be fully absorbed. Conversely, a more buoyant level of aggregate demand would ease these problems of structural unemployment. In the 1950's and 1960's this was one of the main reasons why the labour market was able to adjust to continuous changes on both the supply and demand side. In recent years there has been a "hardening of the arteries" in the labour market, and this has been exacerbated by the lack of aggregate demand. A renewed expansion of aggregate demand will not in itself unblock these arteries, but it will create a better climate for the equilibrating forces of the labour and capital markets to function more effectively.

Because of the importance of determining the factors underlying the increase in unemployment in recent years, and in particular how they might respond to a broadly-based economic recovery, an attempt has been made in an Annex to the present Report, to identify the demand effects and the other more structural causes of present unemployment quantitatively. Given the difficulties already described in identifying these different aspects of increasing unemployment separately, the estimates obviously and of necessity reflect an important element of judgment about which opinions can legitimately differ. Nevertheless, it is felt that an approach along these lines can be useful in guiding the policy debate, especially when framing demand management policies. As the focus of this Report, however, is on medium-term manpower and employment policies, the main analysis of the causes of unemployment in Chapter I of the present Report concentrates on identifying all the various labour market trends, other than the level of economic activity, that are likely to influence unemployment, and on other possible structural imbalances in the labour market.

BROAD POLICY OPTIONS

No matter what the causes of the current high rates of unemployment turn out to be in the final analysis, the effects, in the form of current and future resource wastage and the necessary associated income transfer burdens, are the same. Similarly, but to a lesser extent, so are available policy options. At the broadest policy level, there are four main possible lines of action:
— policies to increase employment,
— policies to reduce labour supply,
— policies to reduce rigidities in wage adjustments to clear labour markets,
— policies to alleviate the economic and social consequences of unemployment.

In addition, manpower adjustment policies can be applied to reduce frictional and mismatch unemployment, e.g. measures facilitating the transition from school to work as well as training, mobility and placement measures. While these

1. See: "A Growth Scenario to 1980", OECD, *Economic Outlook* No. 19, July 1976.

latter measures are of considerable importance for improving the functioning of the labour market, their impact on reducing the aggregate rate of unemployment in the short term will necessarily be limited as long as job vacancies virtually do not exist.

This report is primarily concerned with the first option, i.e. increasing the demand for labour, both globally and selectively, in order to provide jobs for those who are able and willing to work at the going wage rates. Such policies, however, must be responsive to underlying structural trends and must be co-ordinated with appropriate structural policies. This report, therefore, will also deal to a considerable extent with the analysis of structural labour-market trends and policies which are relevant for the formulation of a medium-term strategy.

Since the demand for labour (or any other factor, for that matter) is derived from the demand for the output which that labour produces, it follows that one of the most direct methods of increasing employment is to increase demand for the final output that labour produces. In the most general case, this can be done by increasing aggregate demand. This is the first and most obvious course of action to be pursued to stimulate employment. Buoyant aggregate demand may not always be a sufficient condition for full employment, but it most certainly is a necessary condition. At present and over the foreseeable future, there are three major constraints limiting the ability of governments to stimulate demand sufficiently to absorb the total amount of redundant labour:

— the need to curb inflation;
— the need to achieve balance-of-payments equilibrium;
— the need to constrain public expenditure.

Whether or not these constraints are (or should be) as binding as some Member countries perceive them to be is questionable, but the fact is that policy decisions about these matters have already been taken and it is not part of the mandate of this Report to examine them, except insofar as they provide a context for the policy problems and choices which are examined. In particular, and conditioned by the desire to curb inflation and by the concern about any resurgence of inflation, OECD governments agreed in June 1976 (and reaffirmed their agreement in June 1977) on a medium-term strategy to achieve "economic expansion which is moderate but sustained". Thus, this policy choice at any moment in time does operate as a constraint on the range of policies designed to stimulate employment.

With the severe constraints that there are on expansionary policies, many countries are now seriously considering the second of the above options, which consists of measures intended either to reduce labour-force participation or working time. Unemployment, in this case, would be redistributed to those who can afford or—under certain circumstances—would even prefer to stay out of the labour force for intermittent periods. Alternatively, it would be spread via shorter working hours over the whole, or significant fractions, of the labour force, instead of affecting a small fraction more severely than the rest.

This approach, however, requires that serious consideration be given to the following two issues:

— the concept of a "given" stock of available jobs to be shared is based on a prior and deliberate policy decision on constraining the expansion of aggregate demand and output (under present conditions mainly determined by the concern about inflation);
— redistribution of the burden of unemployment implies an improvement in the welfare of the unemployed by lowering the welfare standards of others.

To the extent that no actual redistribution is accomplished, i.e. that the unemployed are made momentarily better off without other members of the work force being made worse off, there would be more claims and additional inflationary pressures. This result would render the whole strategy a failure since the initial policy choice of limited demand and output growth and, thus, a limited number of available jobs, was dictated by the fear of generating inflationary pressures.

The success of policies to reduce the labour supply in order to combat unemployment, therefore, is crucially dependent on the possibility of achieving a redistribution of welfare. Whether such possibilities exist will depend on many institutional, historical, political and attitude-linked factors. These will vary greatly between countries and there is little wisdom which can be added through economic analysis. Such factors as the prevailing industrial relations system or the amount of social cohesion in a country, or the political skill of the Government, are all relevant. Because of the uncertainty and wide range of these institutional variables, which also vary substantially between countries, the present report cannot examine this policy option in any depth[2].

The third policy option, improving wage adjustments, is based on the view that wage rigidities and difficulties in adjusting wages relative to prices, to other factor costs, or to each other, form one of the major explanations of labour market imbalances. In particular the changing size, growth and composition of the labour force requires—according to this view—more flexible wage adjustments if equilibrium in the labour market, i.e. full-employment, is to be achieved. Consequently, one of the relevant targets of policy intervention is the wage and price determination process. This opens a very wide range of issues such as wage-price dynamics in contemporary economies, the shift in collective bargaining attitudes and objectives, the growing importance of non-labour costs and the increasingly fixed nature of labour costs. On the policy side considerations of job security regulations, incomes policies, income guarantees and transfers are relevant. While some of these issues are dealt with briefly in the present report, it would clearly be beyond its scope and outside the area of manpower and employment policies to cover the whole area of collective bargaining, incomes policy and other measures to influence factor and product prices. This, however, is not meant to imply that this policy option is not regarded as a further essential element for the achievement of full-employment over the medium-term[3].

The fourth broad policy option consists of "living with unemployment". There is no need to expand on why this would be the worst—though unfortunately not the least unlikely—outcome over the medium term. The economic problems associated with prolonged periods of income maintenance are, of course, highly relevant in the present context. However, the mandate for the present report was the policy problem of regaining full employment over the medium term. Therefore, the fourth broad policy option, how to live with unemployment, will not be pursued further.

The following two chapters are intended to provide insight into the main changes which occurred between the 1960's and the 1970's in labour-market trends and policies: Chapter I will deal with the changing structure and functioning of labour markets and will identify a number of significant structural employment problems which will require appropriate policy response over the medium term. Chapter II will analyse the changing emphasis of manpower

2. It also should be borne in mind that many of the measures to reduce labour supply will tend to lead to results which could not easily be reversed later. For some countries at least it cannot be excluded that in the slightly longer term, e.g. after the mid-1980's, there may be a return to problems of slow labour-force growth constraining economic policy and leading to possible labour shortages.
3. A considerable amount of such work is currently being carried out elsewhere in the Organisation. See: *Towards Full Employment and Price Stability,* A report to the OECD by a group of independent experts, OECD 1977.

policies since their implementation in the early sixties and will analyse the current policy dilemma created by the continuing labour market slack. Against this background the succeeding two chapters will reconsider and analyse relevant policy options in relation to a medium-term strategy for employment and manpower policies. Chapter III will examine a number of global and selective measures to raise the demand for labour. Chapter IV will analyse measures required in response to significant structural shifts of the employment system.

Chapter I

THE CHANGING STRUCTURE
AND FUNCTIONING OF LABOUR MARKETS

It was pointed out in the Introduction that the trend of unemployment has been worsening since the late 1960's. Mention was also made of the possibility that the nature of unemployment is changing, both adding to the concern about present levels of unemployment and raising doubts about the effectiveness of present policy instruments in reducing these high levels of unemployment. If structural imbalances in employment have built up in recent years, and are likely to continue, then traditional demand-management policies alone may no longer be a sufficient—albeit a necessary—condition of a return to full employment. The likelihood that the nature of unemployment is changing and is being reflected by a rising trend is further emphasised by the following factors.

The level of unemployment seems to have shifted with cyclical peaks. Some refer to this as the full employment-unemployment level, but in a sense it may be misleading to do so. The cyclical peaks correspond to roughly equivalent demand pressures only in the case of some countries. What is of interest, however, is that a cyclical-peak comparison of unemployment rates does make it possible to observe the rate of unemployment obtained during the "best" performance years in an economy. If over a ten- or fifteen-year period an economy peaks three times, but always below potential capacity, the assumption can nevertheless be made that these peaks represent a "full-employment" level. Whether or not the economy had still greater potential is mainly a question of measurement. Given these limitations, Table 1 illustrates that with few exceptions, the unemployment rate has risen where distinct cyclical peaks are observable. Demand pressures at the various peaks are almost equivalent for Canada, France,

Table 1. **Unemployment rates in cyclical peak years for some OECD countries**

	1960-1965		1966-1970		1971-1976	
U.S.A.			(1966)	3.6	(1973)	4.7
Canada			(1966)	3.5	(1973)	5.6
France	(1964)	1.1	(1969)	1.6	(1973)	2.0
Germany, F.R.	(1965)	0.5	(1970)	0.6	(1973)	1.0
Italy	(1962)	2.9	(1970)	3.1	(1973)	3.4
U.K.	(1964)	1.4			(1973)	2.3
Netherlands	(1965)	0.8	(1969)	1.4	(1973)	2.4
Belgium	(1965)	1.7	(1970)	1.8	(1973)	2.2
Sweden	(1964)	1.6	(1970)	1.5	(1974)	2.0

Source: **OECD,** *Labour Force Statistics.*

15

the United Kingdom and Belgium; the later period for the United States, Germany, Italy and Sweden exhibits a larger gap between actual and potential GDP of about two per cent; and the later periods in the Netherlands represent stronger levels of demand. Whichever way it is wished to interpret the data, there has, however, been a change for the worse in the relationship between the unemployment rate and cyclical peaks. Consequently, each downturn begins with a higher unemployment rate.

The relationship between the level of unemployment and the proportion of unfilled vacancies has also changed over time, for most of the countries with available data, as Diagram 4 of Annex I illustrates. While this in itself does not suggest any causes for the shift, it does again demonstrate that structural changes are occurring in the labour market. Unfortunately, while the vacancy concept is very relevant for analytical purposes, vacancy data are perhaps one of the least reliable sets of labour market data with which analysts have to work, the reasons for this having been recently summed up by Driehuis[1]. To the extent that the data are usable, they show generally that a strong shift occurred for almost every country around 1969-70, although there were exceptions. The conclusion is that when unemployment is rising, vacancies tend to fall less than in previous years (or not at all, or may even rise). This is a disturbing result since it means that an increasing proportion of all new jobs are not having the effect of reducing unemployment, but are remaining unfilled.

In comparing rates of unemployment at the most recent cyclical peaks for nine major OECD countries, the peak unemployment rates have increased on average by 0.8 per cent (unweighted). If the comparison is made only for those five countries where the estimated gap between potential and actual GDP at the two peak periods is similar or smaller, then the increase in peak-year unemployment rises to 1.0 per cent. This figure is an estimate, and should only be considered in conjunction with the fact that unemployment seems to have increased (for several countries) at all levels of capacity utilisation and job vacancies, i.e. demand pressures, suggesting that basic changes have occurred in the labour market. This chapter will focus mainly on an analysis of whether any of these changes can be tracked down to the operation of the labour market itself. The findings indicate that the answer is affirmative.

THE UNEMPLOYMENT LEVEL

Conceptually, there are three quite different factors that lead to a higher aggregate rate of unemployment. The first and most important occurs when the aggregate net labour supply exceeds the aggregate net labour required. The second occurs either because the job openings offered do not match the employment opportunities demanded or the qualifications of those seeking employment. The third results from an increased labour-market throughput which increases the number of "turn-around" or friction points at which a period of unemployment, however short, can take place. The evidence suggests that the current high levels of unemployment are the result of changes in all these situations.

Since the existence of unemployment does not automatically imply that there is an aggregate labour demand shortage—it could be the result of higher flow rates (friction) or structural mismatches—it is important to try to estimate aggregate labour demand and supply in order to estimate the weight of these

1. Wim Driehuis, "Capital-Labour Substitution and Other Potential Determinants of Structural Employment and Unemployment", in: *Structural Determinants of Employment and Unemployment,* Vol. II, OECD, forthcoming.

two components. To determine approximately whether aggregate labour demand and supply are imbalanced, Driehuis has summed actual employment levels and vacancies on the one hand, and the measured labour force plus potential entrants on the other[2]. Diagram 5 of Annex I shows some preliminary results of such an exercise. With the recent exception of France (which had its recessionary downturn after most other countries), the five countries shown have generally been suffering from inadequate demand since the mid or late 1960's. In the case of Canada and the United States, although precise calculations have not been made, it would seem virtually impossible to explain the relatively high unemployment rates without resorting to aggregate supply and demand imbalance factors. The major question, however, is what the causes of the imbalances have been. Have certain shifts occurred which make it increasingly difficult for demand to keep abreast of an ever-growing supply, and will growth be a sufficient answer? Before turning to this question, it is useful to look more closely at the likely medium-term situation with respect to aggregate demand and supply imbalance.

Forecasting future labour demand and supply is a hazardous undertaking, but Table 2 presents the results of one such forecast. The results should only be interpreted as indicating an order of magnitude for the problem of balancing

Table 2. **Annual growth rates of GNP/GDP volume required to absorb incremental labour force; selected OECD countries, 1976-1985**

	Labour force growth		Potential productivity growth[1]	Required GNP/GDP growth	
	1976-1980	1980-1985	1976-1985	1976-1980	1980-1985
Canada	2.3	1.8	2.0	4.3	3.8
United States	2.0	1.3	1.5	3.3	2.8
Japan	0.8	0.8	4.8	5.6	5.6
Germany	0.3	0.6	3.7	4.0	4.3
France	0.8	0.8	3.8	4.6	4.6
Italy	0.8	1.0	3.7	4.5	4.7
United Kingdom	0.5	0.7	1.8	2.3	2.5
Sweden	0.6	0.9	2.2	2.8	3.1

1. The underlying or potential rate of productivity growth assuming a strong expansion of investment consistent with economic recovery.

Source: Secretariat estimates based on various long-term national plans submitted by the Working Party No. 2 of the Economic Policy Committee.

the aggregate levels of labour demand and supply in the medium term. It is clear from these results that a return to full employment places heavy responsibility on economic growth. Also, two assumptions underlying those estimates should be borne in mind. First, it is not assumed that structural shifts will lead to further unemployment. However, our findings of increased cyclical peak unemployment may cast some doubt on the correctness of this assumption. Second, the required growth rates are only those necessary to absorb future additions to the labour supply; they will not cut into present labour surpluses. Consequently, growth rates higher than those shown would be required to reduce both the currenth high levels of unemployment and absorb future labour force growth.

2. Wim Driehuis, "Capital-Labour Substitution", *op. cit.*

CHANGED EMPLOYMENT FACTORS

For the first time in ten years civilian employment in the OECD area in 1975 registered a negative rate of growth (-0.9 per cent over the previous year), to reach a total of 301.6 million persons, thus widening the gap between labour force and employment to 16.5 million persons unemployed. The overall average annual rate of growth of civilian employment for the period 1965-75 is 0.9 per cent in the OECD area, but noticeable differences exist between countries, as illustrated in Diagram 6 of Annex I.

One of the outstanding shifts has been in the structure of sectoral employment. At the beginning of the period (1965) employment in the OECD area was distributed as follows: agriculture 17.3 per cent, industry 36.5 per cent and tertiary 46.2 per cent. At the end of the period (1975) the distribution was 11.8 per cent agriculture, 35.3 per cent for industry and 52.9 per cent for the tertiary sector. During the 1965-75 period employment in the agricultural sector declined at an average rate of 3.1 per cent per year, while employment in the industrial and tertiary sectors increased at annual rates of 0.5 per cent and 2.4 per cent respectively. If the contribution each sector makes to overall employment growth is considered the figures are as in Table 3.

Table 3. **Sectoral contributions to employment growth**

Average annual rate of growth (per cent)	1965-1975	1965-1970	1970-1975
Civilian employment OECD	0.9	1.1	0.8
Contribution of:			
Agriculture	−0.5	−0.5	−0.5
Industry	0.2	0.4	−0.1
Tertiary	1.2	1.2	1.3

Source: OECD, *Labour Force Statistics.*

In the period 1970-75 the tertiary sector was the only sector sustaining employment growth in the OECD (it should be noted, however, that 1975 was a particularly bad year which heavily influenced this average, since 4.4 million jobs disappeared in industry, a drop of 4.1 per cent over 1974).

Diagram 7 of Annex I illustrates the contributions that various sectors have made to employment growth. In almost all OECD countries employment in the tertiary sector has been growing much faster than overall civilian employment, thus compensating for the decrease in agricultural employment and the relative stagnation of the industry sector. Even when measured between peak years in some countries, the percentage of *net* jobs created in the tertiary sector is quite remarkable. For example, in the United States between 1966 and 1973, the tertiary sector was responsible for 92 per cent of net jobs created; in Canada, for the same period, the percentage was 86 per cent. In several years and in various countries, industry growth was actually negative, and tertiary sector growth provided all the new jobs. Within the tertiary sector, the growth of the public sector has accounted on average for perhaps one-third of the growth (in Germany it may have been as high as two-thirds).

The rapid change in employment by sector has given rise to an uneven occupational growth process. The demand for professional, technical, and clerical work has grown rapidly in most countries, while that for operatives and semi-skilled workers has declined absolutely. The uneven shifts in the occupational market are significant, and frequently the high-growth occupations have expanded at rates well above the average, while other occupations are declining absolutely. Since this is happening over short periods of time, it implies that occupational structures are not very stable.

A significant factor in changing market structures has been the growth of voluntary part-time work. In several countries, part-time employment now comprises 15-18 per cent of total employment opportunities, and it has risen by about 5 percentage points in the last decade. Generally, about 75 per cent of the part-time opportunities are filled by women, while male youths take up about another 10-15 per cent of the opportunities.

In virtually every OECD country where data are available (except Germany and, on the evidence of the past two years, this may be changing), the functional relationship between unemployment and vacancies is shifting outwards. Thus, rising unemployment, for instance, is associated with slower decreases of vacancies than was previously the case. If the data are correct then either there is an increasing mismatch between jobs created and jobs demanded—either from a skill or occupational standpoint—or there is a greater flow in labour markets which could create more turn-around unemployment; alternatively, workers are becoming choosier about the type of work demanded.

CHANGED SUPPLY FACTORS

An important factor that should not be overlooked has been the constant growth of the labour force, and particularly its accelerated growth in some countries. Chart 1 of the text and Diagram 8 of Annex I illustrate this accelerated labour force growth, as well as the fact that the population of working age has increased in most OECD countries in the recent past. This has required higher economic growth rates and increased capital accumulation if an increase in unemployment is to be avoided at going real wage rates. The civilian labour force in the OECD area grew at an average annual rate of 1.2 per cent during the period 1965-75, keeping slightly ahead of population growth. However, this global rate masks the considerable disparities between regions and countries. Annual labour force growth in North America (2.3 per cent) has been much higher than in OECD Europe (0.5 per cent) during the 1965-75 period. The growth of the Canadian labour force outpaced all other countries, rising at an annual average of 3.3 per cent, followed by Australia (2.5 per cent) and the United States (2.2 per cent). The labour force has been expanding at 1.0 per cent or less in France, Belgium, the Netherlands, and the United Kingdom. Some European countries have suffered declines; Australia has the highest negative annual rate (-0.8 per cent), followed by Greece (-0.6 per cent), Switzerland (-0.3 per cent), and Italy (-0.1 per cent). In Germany the civilian labour force also declined slightly (-0.2 per cent) and the negative trend would have been more marked had it not been for the rapid influx of foreign workers since 1960.

Accompanying this labour force growth there has been a change in its composition. In most countries labour forces are younger and contain more women (see Table 4), and in general the over-55 age group has declined. In Germany, the youth component has been declining, but this is now in the process of change. Japan has always had a large female component, but this has been on the decline, and in addition Japan now faces a rapidly aging labour force. Because different age/sex components of the labour force have different skills, work experiences, job requirements, and career expectations, a changing composition can introduce strains into the labour market adjustment process.

Table 4. **Females as a percentage of the labour force**

	Average 1965-1970	Average 1970-1975
Canada	30.4	33.5
U.S.A.	35.4	37.8
Germany, F.R.	36.1	36.4
Italy	26.8	27.2
U.K.	34.7	36.4
Australia	30.3	33.0
France	—	35.9
Finland	42.9	44.8
Sweden	38.1	40.9
Japan	39.6	38.2

Source: OECD, *Labour Force Statistics.*

The changing composition has been rendered more complicated by the fact that it has primarily been the result of changing group-specific participation rates, and not as much the result of changes in the composition of the population itself, which generally occur at a slow and more predictable pace. Even in Canada, which in the past decade has had the biggest labour force and population growth, and whose labour force has had to digest an enormous "baby boom", the changed labour force composition is primarily the result of changed participation rates. In the majority of OECD countries, overall participation has increased, and generally this has been accomplished by a rise in female rates, and a fall in male rates (except for teenagers). A noticeable decline in most major countries has been that of the participation of males aged 55 and over. A consequence of observing the changed participation of various labour force groups is that caution should be exercised in forecasting future labour shortages or surpluses on the basis of changing population composition alone. Also, the considerable variation between countries suggests that there is much room for further change in participation rates.

Finally, in Western Europe, migrant labour is an important component of the labour force. In France and Germany, foreign labour represents 9 to 10 per cent of the labour force. Italy, which has been the most important labour exporter, is now giving way to Spain, Portugal, Turkey, Greece and North Africa as the major labour exporters to Western Europe, although movements have substantially slowed down since the recession. Diagram 9 of Annex I provides information on the net flows by labour exporting and importing countries, and clearly illustrates the sensitivity of foreign labour to changing economic conditions.

Perhaps one of the least appreciated, and most difficult to interpret, changes in labour supply has been in its nature or quality. Because of rapidly expanding educational attainments, the current generation in the labour force is considerably better educated than any preceding one, and the change has been substantial and rapid. For example, in the United States, in just seven years (1966-73) the percentage of the labour force having some college education increased by 9 percentage points, and the percentage having 8 years of schooling or less also fell by 9 points. Although it is not clear whether the "quality" of college education has been maintained at the same level, it is likely that this change in the nature of the labour force has had an impact on the type of jobs demanded as well as on the wages paid for certain jobs. The difficult question is whether the jobs offered in the market place have changed their content as quickly, so as to match the rise in occupational aspirations and expectations.

CHANGES IN THE STRUCTURE OF UNEMPLOYMENT

A rise in unemployment resulting from a general cyclical downswing affects virtually all of the labour force, but specific groups such as the young and women are more prone to be hit by unemployment than others. Apart from this cyclical vulnerability, young people and women appear to be disproportionately affected by unemployment on a more permanent basis. In an eight-country comparison, youths and females regularly make up 60-70 per cent of total unemployment, which is in excess of their contribution to the labour force (see Chart 2).

On a cyclical peak-year basis there was not one country among seven surveyed[3] that did not show an increased percentage share of youth (under 25 years) unemployment. The increases were greatest in the United Kingdom and Canada, while Italy has the largest share (64 per cent in 1976), and Germany the smallest (29 per cent in 1976). Some of the inter-country differences are affected by different measurement practices, but rates of change and general magnitudes basically reflect real differences. One would, of course, expect youth's share of total unemployment to rise because it represents an increasing proportion of the labour force (except Germany prior to 1976). But even when relative size is allowed for, the youth group is in the worst position. That is to say, it is not only a matter of a bigger share, but also of increasing youth unemployment rates, i.e. increasing relative to the average rate of unemployment. Where the youth labour force growth has been the greatest—Canada and the United States—it would be difficult to attribute much more than 30-50 per cent of the increased share of youth unemployment to increased numbers of youth in the labour force alone. It should also be kept in mind that while the youth population has increased, participation rates in many countries have either stabilized or fallen over the last 15 years, and consequently this has tended to temper the impact that the larger size alone might have had. In Germany, for example, between 1962 and 1973 the participation rate of the 15-19 age group fell 25 percentage points.

As a rule, it is important to distinguish between the teenage group (19 years and less) and the 20-24 age group. In virtually all countries, the teenage unemployment rate is relatively the highest—frequently 3 or 4 times the prime age rate. But in many countries this situation has at least stabilized. For example, in Canada, which has had a growing youth problem, during the peak years 1966-73, when unemployment climbed by 2 per cent, the relative share and relative rate of unemployment for the teenage group remained virtually unchanged. But for the 20-24 age group, both the rate and share increased considerably. The age/sex dispersion indexes reveal that this example can be generalised to several countries.

In most countries female unemployment rates are higher than male rates, but not as high relatively as youth rates (although in some countries, e.g. France, female youth rates have deteriorated rapidly). In the United Kingdom, Japan and Finland, as three examples, female rates are less than male rates. In fact, the United Kingdom appears to be the only country where prime-age males contribute a larger share to unemployment than they do to the labour force. Over a ten-year period women appear to be improving—if often only slightly— their unemployment positions in the United Kingdom, Sweden, the United States and Australia. In Japan, however, the fall in the female labour force participation rate is contrary to the experience in other countries, and may have been partially responsible for easing pressures on the unemployment rate. But even so, total

---

3. There were no comparable peak years for Japan.

Chart 2

UNEMPLOYMENT PERCENTAGE DISTRIBUTION BY AGE AND SEX
IN RECENT PEAK YEARS AND 1976

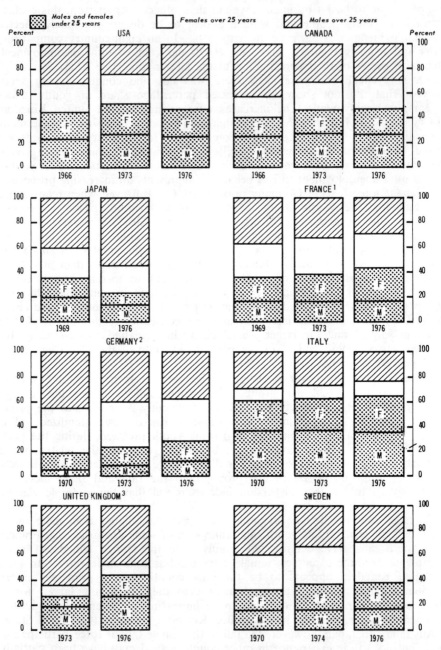

1. March of each year.
2. End of September.
3. Great Britain only : January and July data.

Source : OECD Labour Force Statistics and National Sources.

22

Chart 3
INDEX OF UNEMPLOYMENT DISPERSION BY AGE AND SEX[1]

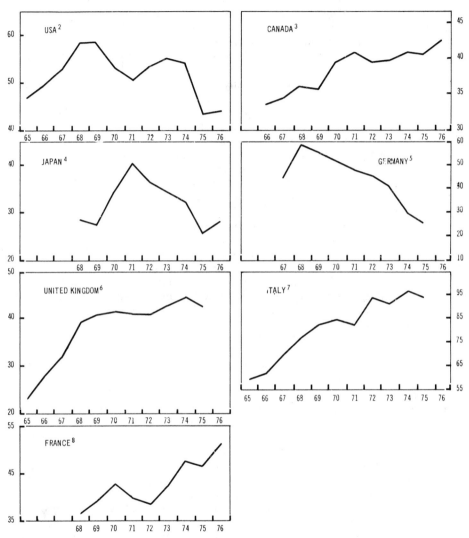

1. The dispersion index is calculated by summing the absolute difference between the share in unemployment and its share in the labour force for each sex age group.
2. USA : 4 age groups : 16-19, 20-24, 25-54, 55 years and over.
3. CANADA : Males : 3 age groups 15-24, 25-54, 55 years and over. Females : 2 age-groups 15-24, 25 years and over.
4. JAPAN : 4 age groups : 15-19, 20-24, 25,54, 55 years and over.
5. GERMANY : 4 age groups : 15-19, 20-24, 25-54, 55 years and over. End of September.
6. UNITED KINGDOM : 3 age groups : 16-19, 20-24, 25 years and over.
7. ITALY : 4 age groups : 15-19, 20-24, 25-54, 55 years and over.
8. FRANCE : 3 age groups : under 25, 25-49 50 years and over.

Sources : OECD Labour Force Statistics and National Sources.

female employment has steadily increased. In Canada, Finland, Germany and Italy, the employment situation for women has been deteriorating, but as already noted, in Finland women are relatively better off to begin with, and in Germany recent trends seem more favourable[4].

Charts 3 and 4 illustrate more concisely much of what has been said above concerning the contributions to unemployment that specific groups make. The diagrams represent weighted unemployment dispersion indexes for seven countries that illustrate the difference between a specific group's contribution to unemployment and its contribution to the labour force. The summation of individual group differences (disregarding sign) provides a weighted dispersion index. The data show that on an age/sex breakdown, the index for Canada, the United Kingdom, Italy and France has persistently worsened. For Japan and Germany the index is improving, and for the United States (where race has been included in other versions) it is currently improving but it has a ten-year history of fluctuation (data limitations only allowed us to calculate indices up to 1975). The worsening dispersions suggest that increasing labour market segmentation is occurring along age and sex lines, and especially the former—that is, advantaged groups with favourable dispersions are improving their positions and groups with negative dispersions are becoming even worse off in terms of access to employment. However, the indices do not explain why the dispersions are becoming worse, where this is the case. Certain groups may either be voluntarily opting for unemployment, or they may indeed be finding it increasingly difficult to gain access to labour markets and to maintain employment. There is much other information to support the latter explanation. For Canada, Germany and the United States it was also possible to construct dispersion indices for unemployment by occupation, and the results showed a constantly improving situation. In Canada, a country with a considerable regional unemployment problem, the dispersion index also indicates an improving situation, whereas in the United States it has worsened.

An analysis of unemployment by occupation is restricted to a few countries because of data limitations. Also, the different classification procedures make inter-country comparisons hazardous. For example, in Germany, one of the fastest-growing occupational categories is unskilled labour, yet in Canada this category registers a strong decline. Is this a real or a statistical difference? But the data for countries where they are available show that workers are moving in the "right" directions. High-growth, low-unemployment occupations (professional and technical, clerical), have in general registered slightly increasing unemployment rates, whereas slow-growth, high-unemployment occupations have sometimes registered slower relative increases in their rates of unemployment. If anything, this behaviour suggests that workers are moving into the fast-growth occupations. Thus, supply side-pressure is increasing the unemployment rates somewhat. Dispersion indices for several occupations in the United States, Germany and Canada show dispersion diminishing over time. While, therefore, the direction of change is favourable, a faster movement from high-unemployment to low-unemployment occupations would tend to reduce aggregate unemployment rates.

Generally, the structure of unemployment by duration has become worse. Chart 5 illustrates data on unemployment according to duration of search for six industrial countries. Table 5 shows for these countries that the rate of long-duration unemployment (over 26 weeks, or 6 months) doubled between the periods 1965-70 and 1970-75.

---

4. For a more extended analysis of the effects of the 1973-75 recession on the labour-market experience of women in selected OECD Member countries, see *The 1974-75 Recession and the Employment of Women*, OECD, 1976.

Chart 4

AGE AND SEX SPECIFIC UNEMPLOYMENT DISPERSION

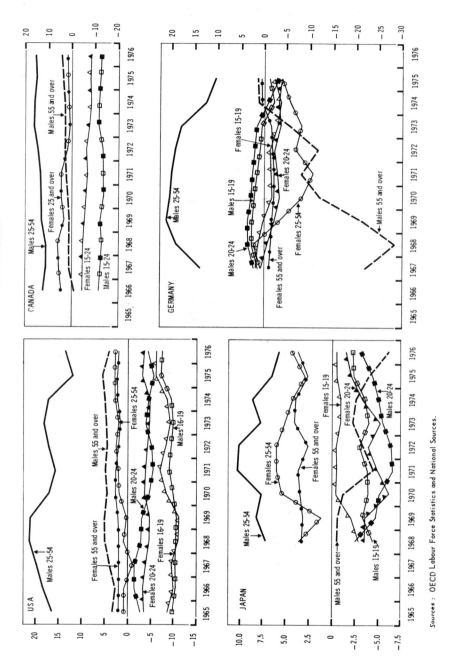

Sources : OECD Labour Force Statistics and National Sources.

25

Chart 4 (continued)

AGE AND SEX SPECIFIC UNEMPLOYMENT DISPERSION[1]

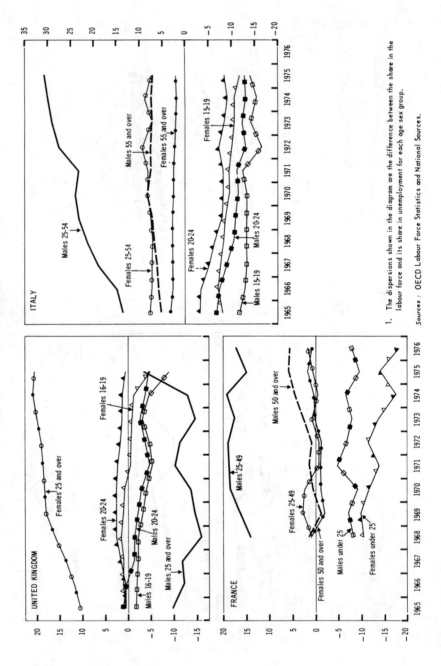

1. The dispersions shown in the diagram are the difference between the share in the labour force and its share in unemployment for each age sex group.

Sources : OECD Labour Force Statistics and National Sources.

26

Chart 5

DURATION OF UNEMPLOYMENT

(percentage distribution of unemployed by duration of search)

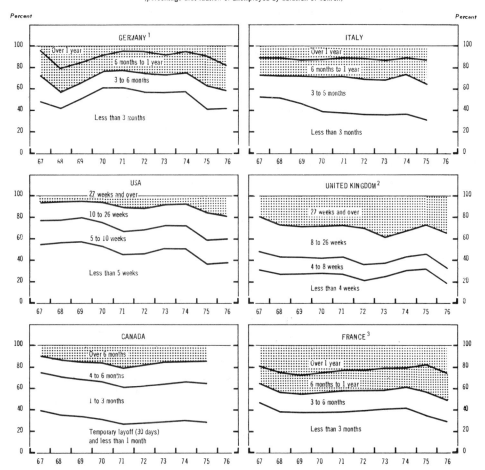

1. End of September of each year.
2. Great Britain only.
3. PDRES* only. March of each year.

* Population disponible à la recherche d'un emploi salarié.

Sources : National Sources.

Table 5. **The rate of long-duration unemployment in six countries as a percentage of the total labour force**

	1965-1970	1970-1975
U.S.A. (over 26 weeks)	0.3	0.6
Canada (over 6 months)	0.6	1.0
Germany, F.R. (over 6 months)	0.2[1]	0.4
U.K. (over 27 weeks)	0.5	0.8
Italy[2]	1.4	1.5
France (over 6 months)	0.5	0.8

1. Average 1967-1970.
2. In Italy the rates become 0.5 and 0.4 if school-leavers are excluded.
Sources: National sources.

27

It is to be expected that duration will increase with the level of unemployment. In Canada, long-duration unemployment has increased substantially. For example, between the peak years 1966-73 the average duration increased from 10 to 13 weeks, and explains one-half of the increase in aggregate unemployment over this period. The other half is explained by an increased number of spells of unemployment. However, it is disturbing that in those countries where long-duration unemployment has declined or stabilized, it coincides with a fall in the participation rate of older workers. Consequently, one suspects that long-duration unemployment is underestimated because older workers may be dropping out of the labour force after a long spell of unemployment. And the fact that this downward trend in the participation of older workers is uninterrupted suggests that they are not re-entering the labour force. During the peak years 1966-73, in the United States, the average duration of unemployment fell very slightly even though aggregate unemployment rose. Closer examination, however, reveals that much of this was due to a fall in the long-term unemployment of males 45 years and over, which in turn was matched by a fall in their participation rates. In France, between the peak years 1969-74, average duration fell slightly, but only because of a drop in the 50-year-and-over group's six-month or longer rate of unemployment (all other age groups showed an increased duration). Moreover, this reduction was accompanied by a 4 point drop in this group's labour force participation rate. Generally, long-duration unemployment correlates positively with age, but shows no significant difference with regard to sex.

There is very little information on the pre- and post-labour force status of the stock of unemployed. Data on pre-unemployment status would tell us the numbers seeking employment for the first time, those who voluntarily left employment, and those who were dismissed. Data on the subsequent status of the unemployed would indicate the numbers leaving unemployment through finding a job or, alternatively, by withdrawing from the active labour force. In the United States during the peak years 1966-73 the entire increase in unemployment can be explained by the relative rise of those workers who have been dismissed. The groups representing first job seekers and voluntary job-leavers have fallen relatively—although together they still comprise the largest number of unemployed. A special United States survey covering the years 1968-75 reveals that one-third of the males, and over one-half of the females quite regularly complete a spell of unemployment by withdrawing from the labour force[5]. Significantly, the labour force withdrawals are correlated with age and duration, which supports the above findings concerning duration and participation rates. In Canada, comparing the period 1963-1973, it was shown that the number of first job seekers was up as a proportion of the total unemployed, as was the percentage of unemployed ending their spell by withdrawing from the labour force. In France, the percentage of unemployed due to dismissal between 1965-76 increased from 32 per cent to 45 per cent, although on a peak-to-peak basis there was not much change. In Italy, first job seekers have risen as a percentage of total unemployed from 35 per cent in 1965 to 62 per cent in 1975. The evidence is fragmentary, but it all points in one direction: availability of employment has worsened in comparison to the strong influx of job seekers, and dismissals also are playing a more important role.

It is sometimes contended that unemployment does not impose such economic hardship today because fewer of the unemployed are heads of households. On the same basis it is also argued that the weaker connection to the labour market of secondary family workers is a potential source of increased job-search

5. S. Garfinkle, "The Outcome of a Spell of Unemployment", *Monthly Labour Review,* Volume 100, January 1977.

unemployment. Whether or not these conclusions follow, the data do show that fewer of the unemployed are heads of household—but the evidence is confined to the United States and Canada. In Canada, between 1961 and 1973 the percentage of unemployed consisting of heads of household fell from 55 per cent to 44 per cent, and in the United States over the period 1963-73 the percentage fell from 40 per cent to 34 per cent.

CHANGES IN THE COST OF LABOUR

An increase in the cost of labour relative to the cost of capital or relative to the value of output can affect the creation of employment opportunities in the longer run. The following findings are preliminary. Table 6 presents the results of one study that compares the relative user costs of labour and capital and which might therefore serve as a guide to the possibility that employment opportunities are being limited by the substitution of capital for labour. On the labour cost side, wage rates and other compensations are included, while on the capital cost side, equipment cost and rate of interest are included. Because no allowance has been made for changing depreciation costs and risk premia on the one hand, and capital tax incentives and subsidies on the other, the full user cost of capital is not actually calculated. However, these two exclusions move in offsetting directions, so that the calculated relative cost ratios should be roughly representative. The data in Table 6 show that in Germany, France, Italy, the Netherlands, and Belgium, there has been a greater rise in wage costs than in capital costs. In Germany and Italy, relative wage costs appear to weaken after 1970. In France, the movement levels off in the mid-1960's, and the Netherlands and Belgium show continuing labour cost increases.

Table 6. **Index of ratio of wage costs to capital cost 1955-1974**
1955-1957 = 100

	Three-year average				
	1955-1957	1959-1961	1963-1965	1967-1969	1971-1973
Germany, F.R.	100	129	174	203	219
France	100	127	165	163	166
United Kingdom	100	96	110	101	97
Italy	100	142	161	204	216
Netherlands	100	116	125	135	163
Belgium	100	94	108	119	137

Source: Driehuis, op. cit.

Because of the difficulties in interpreting these data concerning the relative costs of labour and capital, and also because it is uncertain how far capital-labour substitution is technically feasible even in the longer run, any conclusions must be heavily qualified. Professor Driehuis suggests that in Germany, Italy, the Netherlands and Belgium, "where substitution is relevant and possible", it is not unreasonable to think that investment in capital has been directed to rationalisation (cost-reduction) rather than to enlargement of capacity. This conclusion is generally supported by a review of the increases in labour productivity in various OECD Member countries following periods in which relative labour costs had risen rapidly. Thus the rise in relative labour costs in the mid-1960's was followed by accelerated productivity increases in the last half of the 1960's in France, Germany and the United Kingdom, suggesting some displacement of labour by capital.

As to the question of changes in real wages alone during the decade 1963-74, there is evidence of an acceleration (real average earnings per man hour in manufacturing) in Germany, Italy, and the United States in the 1960's; no acceleration in Canada, Sweden and the United Kingdom; and unclear evidence for France and the Netherlands. What is more important in this context, however, is the movement of unit labour costs relative to the value of output, which will also be affected by changes in productivity. In a number of countries there may have been some longer-term decline in profitability as real wages increased relative to the value of output, and by more than can be accounted for by cyclical movements in productivity. This has led an independent OECD Expert Group to conclude that "profitability has probably declined in the United States, Germany, Italy and the United Kingdom, among the major countries, and in Belgium and the Netherlands, among the smaller countries reviewed"[6].

This decline in profitability, combined with some pessimism concerning longer-run growth prospects has led to stagnating investment. As a result, a situation is now developing in some countries where the available capital stock is insufficient to support traditional levels of high employment at going real wage rates. An indication of the magnitude of this problem is provided in Annex II where estimates are given of the unemployment which might be attributed to capital shortages. These estimates suggest that the potential problem of "capital-shortage" unemployment is already significant and increasing, and while economic recovery can itself be expected to encourage some of the investment needed to avoid future bottlenecks, other more direct measures to induce investment and to adjust relative prices may also be required.

IS LABOUR TENDING TO BECOME A FIXED COST?

There is another aspect of labour cost that is perhaps as relevant to the level of unemployment as the issue of labour costs is relative to capital costs, and this is whether labour is being increasingly regarded by enterprises as a fixed or quasi-fixed factor. Enterprises generally operate with a margin of unused capacity (or labour slack) in order to accommodate expected but uncertain cyclical or seasonal increases, or relatively unexpected increases in demand for output. It is reasonable to assume that the size of this margin will vary with the cost of labour relative to output price, as well as with the economic costs incurred by dismissing slack labour should actual output fall materially short of that expected. This type of behaviour which is frequently called labour hoarding, or labour stocking, is separate from the question of capital substitution, at least in a short or medium-term time perspective. Unavoidable fixed costs associated with releasing slack labour—both hiring (e.g. training costs), and dismissal costs (e.g. redundancy payments)—determine to what extent an enterprise regards its labour input as a quasi-fixed investment. And to the extent to which labour is viewed as such, the more cautious enterprises will be in hiring new labour as they attempt to reduce the margin required for expansion. Firms will take on new labour only when the degree of certainty is much higher concerning output expansion and that it will also be sustained for a significant period.

According to recent research by the Secretariat there is considerable evidence to show that the fixed element of labour costs has grown over time. As a result, total labour costs have become less sensitive to changes in output, and unit labour

6. *Towards Full Employment and Price Stability, op. cit.*, pp. 156-167, and especially para. 237.

costs can now be expected to rise more than usual when output declines and less than usual when output increases. Tentative estimates suggest that the more than proportionate rise in fixed labour costs between the mid-1960's and the mid-1970's has added 0.5-0.9 per cent to the rise in unit labour costs ordinarily associated with a 10 per cent fall in output. Conversely, the rise in unit labour costs should be correspondingly lower when output increases. As regards employment, a larger proportion of fixed labour costs implies smaller adjustments in response to a given change in output. The available evidence reveals a growing role for certain elements of internally-created fixed employment costs, reflecting both human capital considerations and a stronger demand for leisure and improved working conditions. At the same time, several countries seem to have witnessed a rise in the fixed component of statutory contributions to social security payable by employers. Unlike increases in privately incurred fixed costs, this does not necessarily imply a lowering of the propensity of employers to dismiss labour in times of economic depression. But when output recovers, a higher component of fixed costs within social security contributions may stimulate the use of overtime work thereby raising productivity (output per employed person) by larger than normal amounts.

A particularly important element of the fixed nature of labour has been the rise of dismissal costs in several countries during the recent recession. In Italy most lay-offs must be justified, and employer and trade union organisations can appeal decisions before tribunals. The Dismissal Protection Act in Germany also restrains employers from dismissing workers except for certain reasons, and long-term employees have been able to secure up to 18 months' pay upon being laid off. In France, various ordinances and Acts limit the rights of dismissal, and provide for redundancy payments. In the Netherlands, statutory redundancy payments can total up to two and one-half years' pay. In Britain, statutory redundancy payments can amount to 30 weeks' wages, although the company can often retrieve half of this amount from the Redundancy Fund. In Canada legislation is not as strong and frequently applies only to required periods of advance notice of large lay-offs; but many collective agreements contain seniority and severance pay provisions as well as other employment guarantee measures.

In addition to the evidence earlier reported for France, there has also been evidence of a labour "shake-out" in the United Kingdom[7]. Also, a recent OECD study[8] devoted to an analysis of the efficacy of employment security measures during the recent recession in the United Kingdom, France and Germany, suggests among other things that the protection of existing labour force members has increased markedly in recent years.

THE LIBERALISATION OF UNEMPLOYMENT INSURANCE SCHEMES

Since considerable public attention has been drawn to this issue it is appropriate to review its possible implications for the level of unemployment (however, leaving aside the demand-stabilising effects). The effect of unemployment insurance is to put a floor under the price of non-work and thus raise the supply price of labour services. This can be interpreted as a reduced willingness of workers to accept available employment quickly, either by encouraging job search for better employment, or by encouraging people to shun work

7. This is discussed by A. J. Brown "UV Analysis", in *The Concept and Measurement of Involuntary Unemployment,* ed. C.D.N. Worswick, London: Allen and Unwin, 1976, Chapter 7.
8. John Gennard, *Job Security and Industrial Relations,* OECD, forthcoming.

until benefits lapse. But unemployment insurance may also extend the duration of unemployment of those who expect they are not going to be rehired until the next upswing. That is, expanded insurance benefits and coverage can simply turn former discouraged workers into unemployed workers until benefits run out. In this case, no substantial change has been caused by unemployment benefits; rather, workers are simply shifted from one status to another in the labour force. Unfortunately, the studies of the impact of unemployment insurance never clearly determine which type of unemployment is being created by the increased benefits. If it is the last type, it poses a policy problem of defining priorities in job creation; if it is the first type involving job search, then the increased search may lead partially to longer-term benefits to the economy. It is clearly the first type —"work-shunning" behaviour—that is of immediate concern.

Prior to the reforms of unemployment compensation systems following the 1974/75 recession, the rate at which unemployment insurance replaced lost disposable income varied for married recipients from 60 per cent in the United States and Sweden to 83 per cent in Canada (in a six-country study). The question is, what kind of effect does this alternate income source have on the three possible types of unemployment described above? The answer is in two parts: first, a look at the econometric studies on the subject; and second, some observations designed to question the impacts estimated.

It should be stressed that the econometric evidence applies to insurance schemes before the 1974-75 reforms, but if they had an impact before, then it can be assumed that liberalising reforms would raise the impact estimates some-what. A survey of seven econometric studies covering Canada, the United States and the United Kingdom, shows rather divergent results for the United States which are difficult to interpret (ranging from an impact of +0.2 per cent to 1.2 per cent); for Canada the 1971 reform was estimated to have increased unemployment by about 0.8 per cent in two studies[9]; and in the United Kingdom a study indicated a 0.6 per cent increase in unemployment due to redundancy payments and the earnings-related supplement. However, a United Kingdom government study placed the figure at +0.3 per cent.

Two conclusions emerge from these studies: first, measuring the impact is a difficult process and even then it is not certain which type of unemployment is being created; second, the likely estimated effects appear small. It should also be noted that most studies estimate the gross, and not the net impact of unemployment insurance on the level of unemployment. In fact, insurance benefits, by sustaining purchasing power will often sustain jobs that would otherwise disappear. Moreover, benefits have the advantage of automatically being targeted to high-unemployment areas where the added purchasing power is most needed.

SUMMARY AND FINDINGS

It must be stressed that the findings of this chapter are preliminary and in many cases supported by only limited empirical evidence drawn from a relatively small number of countries. Nonetheless, they have been selected from a number of competing explanations, because they do appear to throw new light on to a broad range of issues. These explanations are largely rooted in the operation of the labour market, and therefore do not explain all of the changes in unemployment. In addition to the statistical material presented in the previous section,

---

9. Although a government review of seven studies estimates the net employment effect at about one half of this level.

a more thorough and detailed analysis has been carried out for a few OECD countries (Canada, France, Germany, Japan, and the USA). This material is not presented because of space limitations, but the following findings are also drawn from these studies.

Level of Unemployment

The non-cyclical increase in the level of unemployment has occurred partially because labour-market shifts have caused imbalances between levels of aggregate labour supply and demand, three factors having played a role: (1) a constantly growing and changing labour supply; (2) changes in the cost and fixed nature of the labour factor of production; (3) labour-market shifts that have increased inflationary pressures which, in turn, have partially induced policy makers to run a tighter economy. The secular increase in unemployment is also likely to have occurred because at every level of aggregate supply and demand there is an increase in gross labour flows which increase the likelihood of unemployment, if even for a short spell. These four trends are dealt with in turn.

i) *Labour supply factors*

One plausible partial explanation for the growing gap between aggregate labour demand and supply centres is the changing process of employment creation. One of the problems of the last decade, marked by the constant growth of employment in the OECD area (except in 1975), was the failure to catch up with an ever-increasing supply. However, a close examination of the French economy during the expansionary period 1968-73 when employment creation exceeded labour force growth, and unemployment actually rose, perhaps provides an explanation that can be generalised to some other OECD countries. The explanation is centred on a series of assumptions, that in varying degrees seem to be supported by these findings. A key element is the fact that labour force growth in most countries where it has occurred has been more the result of increased female participation than of population growth. Another important element is the nature of the current growth process, and more precisely that it is led by the tertiary sector which recruits a large proportion of its new employees from among those outside the ranks of the unemployed. This is because the tertiary sector hires a greater proportion of women than does the industry sector. The industry sector on the other hand recruits a greater proportion from the ranks of the unemployed. What appeared to happen in France was that the tertiary sector brought more people into the labour force, some of whom subsequently became unemployed, than the industry sector recruited from the ranks of the unemployed. Consequently, even though employment creation was substantial, it created jobs primarily for people outside the recorded labour force and unemployment did not fall. The likelihood of this having actually occurred is further enhanced by the fact that tertiary sector employment has higher turnover rates than the industry sector, so it creates more frictional unemployment per unit of employment creation.

What may also be adding to the unemployment problem over time as the tertiary sector expands is that the new recruits—mostly females and teenagers— may no longer be leaving the labour force in such large proportions as during previous down-swings. Because of changed career aspirations and liberalised unemployment assistance these workers, who would at one time have been considered "peripheral" labour, now stay in the labour force to be counted as unemployed. Consequently the nature of the employment growth process itself sows the seeds of higher unemployment: employment creation decreasingly reduces existing unemployment and also generates additional unemployment among the former peripheral labour force. Therefore, as the tertiary sector grows, and the former peripheral labour force becomes increasingly part of the permanent labour force, the gap between aggregate labour demand and supply may persist even in the face of strong employment growth. This explanation must be interpreted carefully. To the extent that new tertiary employees were discouraged workers—and most would have to be considered that—the recorded increases in unemployment do not represent a real, as distinct from a measured, increase in unemployment if one considers that the discouraged workers may also, in fact, be considered as "unemployed". What this process has done is to change the composition of those entering employment and by so doing perhaps increase the duration of unemployment as well.

Labour-exporting countries face a structural shift in their labour forces of a different nature that makes it difficult for aggregate labour demand to match supply. This shift has been brought about recently by the slowdown in economic growth of the labour-importing countries combined with policies designed to discourage labour inflow. Consequently, the former labour-exporting countries not only face the current world recession which affects aggregate labour demand, but they also face a structural shift on the supply side[10].

ii) *Factors affecting the cost of labour*

As we have noted, the analysis is rather inconclusive as to whether the relative cost of labour has increased, and if so, if it has led to a substitution of capital for labour. The available evidence suggests that perhaps this has been the case for Germany, France and the United Kingdom during the later part of the 1960s. There is, however, another possible substitution effect resulting from relative wage increases, and relating to changes in the relative prices of various types of labour. It is possible that there has been a substitution of lower-priced labour—chiefly female—for higher-priced male labour. Moreover, this may have taken place through the increased use of fixed-term contracts, which allow enterprises to escape many of the fixed costs of labour. What appears as crowding older workers out of the labour market is consistent with this substitution effect.

The increased costs of hiring and dismissing labour have undoubtedly turned it into more of a quasi-fixed factor than formerly. This being so there are three impacts on unemployment that could result. First, because of rapid changes in hiring or dismissal costs (e.g. as the result of legislation) there may be an immediate shake-out of labour, and unemployment rises. Second, the process of reducing the enterprise's labour stock may take place through attrition so that the effect on unemployment is more gradual as employers do not hire as much replacement labour, which, of course, increases job-access problems for new entrants. Third, if enterprises operate with smaller labour stocks it no doubt means that they meet an uncertain expansion of output partially by hiring fixed-term labour. The effect of this would be increased gross flows and more unemployment spells for a growing number of workers. Another factor related to the question of fixity is that it gives to labour a status similar to that of a capital investment so that firms have to look at the long-term profitability of each new recruit. In the present situation, with the medium-term economic outlook rather uncertain, firms are likely to show an increased reluctance to make fixed

---

10. These matters are dealt with more extensively in other ongoing work of the Organisation. See: *Migration, Growth and Development,* Report by a Group of Independent Experts, OECD, forthcoming.

investments—in either capital or labour. This again can have serious consequences for new labour-force entrants. One general method for stimulating labour demand would be to reduce the fixity of the labour component; but then this conflicts with the security that this fixity gives to the already employed.

The review of unemployment insurance suggests that it probably has had some effect on increasing unemployment. However, it is not always clear in what manner it does so. To the extent that it simply transforms what would formerly have been discouraged workers into unemployed workers (in order to qualify for improved benefits) it may largely represent a "statistical" increase in unemployment—although the policy implications may be different.

iii) *The labour market and inflation*

It is quite likely that a number of changes in labour markets have resulted in the process of wage and price fixing becoming inherently more inflationary at any given pressure of demand or level of unemployment, and that this is partly responsible for policy-induced constraints on the expansion of aggregate demand. First, and perhaps most importantly, a decline in the money illusion has led wage-earners to bargain for real wage increases, frequently supported by schemes for wage indexation, and this has reduced the scope for adjusting real wage costs by increasing output prices relative to nominal wage rates in the context of economic expansion[11]. Secondly, and as already noted, there is a concern that currently-installed capacity may be insufficient to support traditional levels of full-employment at the going wage rate, so that there is a risk of any rapid upswing being aborted by inflationary bottlenecks. In this situation, demand management is constrained to follow a more moderate course which allows time for and encourages an increase in the capital stock necessary to sustain full employment.

Thirdly, there is the possibility that the changing structure of our economies towards the tertiary industries has led to a reduction in long-run productivity, not matched by wage demands, and thus increased the underlying rate of inflation. As noted earlier, real wages in manufacturing only accelerated in the United States, Germany, and Italy during the 1960s; but the shift of employment to the tertiary sector does not require wage acceleration. Although the statistical analysis is preliminary for the three above countries surveyed, it was established that in each case two relationships held over a number of years: first, productivity changes in the tertiary sector were less than changes in industrial productivity; second, wages in the tertiary sector maintained a relatively fixed relationship with wages in the industry sector. However, tertiary-sector real wages cannot keep pace with changes in the industry sector when its productivity is not growing at the same rate, unless it pushes up money wages disproportionately which, in turn, will create inflationary pressure. The only other way the industrial-tertiary sector wage relationship could remain virtually fixed over time would be if some of the real income associated with the productivity gains in the industry sector were transferred to the tertiary sector, as for example, through public tax and subsidy mechanisms.

The employment shift from industry to tertiary in itself, without further wage push or acceleration can consequently lead to further inflationary pressures as more and more workers enter the lower-productivity tertiary sector and strive to maintain the fixed wage relationship with the industry sector. Chart 6 shows the likely effect that the shift to the tertiary sector has on overall productivity

---

11. For an empirical discussion of real wage bargaining see *Public Expenditure Trends,* OECD, forthcoming.

growth.   The relation between the two variables may not imply a causation, but
the results are rather striking.   What it means, if the two variables are related,
is that people will either have to voluntarily accept smaller increases in real income
as the tertiary sector expands, or else that in order to curb otherwise constant
inflationary pressures (which lead to policy-induced reductions in aggregate
demand) they will have to accept some form of price and income control.   The

Chart 6

PRODUCTIVITY AND TERTIARY SECTOR EMPLOYMENT, OECD 1975

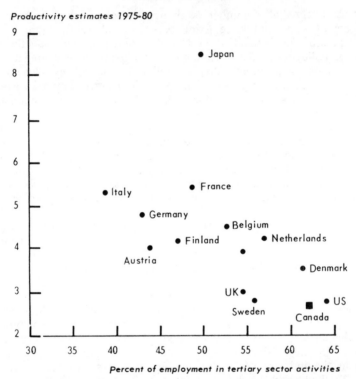

Productivity estimates 1975-80

Percent of employment in tertiary sector activities

Source : OECD, Expenditure Trends in OECD Countries, 1960-1980, Paris,
July 1972, and the OECD observer, No. 74, March-April 1975.
Published in R.A. Jenness «Manpower and Employment
Problems and Prospects» OECD, forthcoming.

major criticism of the above interpretation of the shift to tertiary employment is
that productivity in its true sense is extremely difficult to measure in the tertiary
sector, and that the low recorded increases seriously under-estimate the real
increases.   In this interpretation, therefore, the wage gains in the tertiary sector
may not exceed the real productivity gains and therefore there is little or no
inflationary pressure generated from this source, assuming also that the relevant
price indices adjust to the real productivity increases.

iv) *Increased gross flows in the labour market*

An increase in gross flows of people in and out of the labour force will not directly affect the aggregate stock of labour demand or supply of labour as in the first three factors examined above. An increase in flows will probably lead to an increased number of unemployment spells—some voluntary, others not—which in turn raises the level of unemployment at all levels of demand and supply. Unfortunately, most countries do not publish adequate gross flow data, and consequently many of the questions concerning employment problems can only be guessed at. The importance of a knowledge of gross flows was illustrated in particular for France[12]. It is important to know both the volume and the directions of gross flows: for example, out of a net addition of one million new jobs, how many jobs were eliminated? What was the sectoral and regional balance, i.e. were the jobs created similar to those eliminated, and in the same region? How many workers occupy the same job in a year, i.e. what is the turnover rate by sector or industry? What percentage of new jobs were filled from the ranks of the unemployed as compared to those previously outside the labour force? Are there changes in the numbers of dismissed workers who enter the ranks of the unemployed and those who withdraw from the labour force? How many workers voluntarily quit employment to search for a better job? It soon becomes apparent that the usual labour force information in the form of net stocks measured at time intervals is inadequate to answer basic questions of this kind which require an analysis of the size and nature of gross flows.

An important question surrounds the issue of whether the changing nature of gross flows has been responsible for increasing the level of unemployment. If gross flows have increased has this been the result of voluntary worker actions? It has been possible to approch this question with the help of an analysis of the French labour market[13], and some of the results seem general enough to apply to other countries. Several pieces of evidence were given in support of the belief that gross flows, notably into the labour force, have increased. First, the expanding tertiary sector recruits more from outside the labour force than from the ranks of the recorded unemployed, thus increasing flows for any given level of net employment expansion. Second, there is more intra-sector mobility in the tertiary sector. Third, there is more part-time and fixed-term work in general. Fourth, inter-firm mobility has increased as measured by the length-of-service attachment to a particular firm. Fifth, there has been much decentralisation of economic activity requiring geographical shifts in job requirements and an uneven pattern of job creation and elimination. Sixth, during the period 1968-74, the margin of expansion within enterprises, which is the amount of increased output that can be handled without hiring new labour, fell from 10 per cent to 6 per cent. As a result of these changes therefore, it is likely that gross flows of a significant number of workers have increased, and with each "turnaround" presented an opportunity for a spell of unemployment[14].

The related question is whether this increased flow activity was voluntary. The answers are somewhat circumstantial in nature, but the likelihood is that it was not primarily voluntary. First, the growth of the service sector is beyond individual worker control. Second, the location of industry is also beyond individual worker control. Third, the dishoarding of labour, while perhaps prompted by collective worker action, has been an enterprise, not a worker

12. R. Salais, "Analysis of the Mechanisms Determining Unemployment", in *Structural Determinants of Employment and Unemployment,* Vol. II, OECD, forthcoming.
13. R. Salais, *op. cit.*
14. Though for some, i.e. those protected by security provisions, turnover may have fallen.

decision. Fourth, the increased use of part-time and fixed-term contract labour (partially in response to the dishoarding of more permanent labour) is an enterprise decision, although some workers probably prefer service attachment, and the increased recorded inter-firm mobility is not likely to be all voluntary (e.g. job search), for two reasons: an increase in long-duration, and a decrease in short-duration unemployment does not accord easily with a voluntary job leaving explanation; nor does the increasing proportion of unemployment consisting of dismissals support a voluntary job leaving theory.

On the basis of the evidence for France it would appear that changes in the level of gross flows can partially explain increased levels of unemployment, and that detailed knowledge of the nature of the changes can permit a determination of the causes of unemployment, particularly as to whether they are voluntary or not. Increased gross flows in themselves are likely to cause more "turnaround" unemployment, which if combined with increasing labour market segmentation can lead to long-term unemployment. No attempt is made at this time to generalise the results, but from the foregoing account of gross flows it would appear that similar results might be obtained for other countries. From a policy standpoint the question is whether this type of unemployment resulting from increased flows is accepted as the normal consequence of a dynamic economy, i.e. frictional unemployment, or whether it is regarded as an undesirable consequence of economic activity, and therefore attempts should be made to change the various factors making for increased flows.

Other employment problems

At this stage it is only possible to make some very preliminary and brief observations about the other medium-term employment problems.

The problem of unemployment duration, as distinct from the level of unemployment, has been touched on earlier. All that needs to be stressed here is that the increase in duration in most countries may not be totally reversible, because there is evidence that older workers who have suffered long-duration unemployment withdraw from the labour force. Declining participation rates also suggest that they are not getting back into the labour force. Furthermore, preliminary results from research in the United Kingdom[15] suggest that the job vacancy rate not only corresponds to the level of unemployment, but also to the duration and structure of unemployment. These results suggest that the long-term unemployed virtually become ineligible for future job vacancies, demonstrating again that the unemployment process may be somewhat irreversible.

The fact that the percentage of unemployment consisting of first job-seekers is so high, plus the evidence from our dispersion indices, suggests that labour market segmentation is increasing, especially along age/sex lines. But further examination reveals that it is primarily by age, especially the 20-24 age group (both sexes) and males 55 years and over. However, women also have poorer access to labour markets than males in general (if unemployment rates can be used as a measure), except in the United Kingdom, Japan and Finland, but either position seems to be improving more rapidly than that of the youth group. Undoubtedly, many of the access problems are a result of the economic slowdown, but at least for the 20-24 age group their situation has deteriorated between economic peaks as well. An interesting calculation for United States data reveals that even if the unemployment rate of prime-age white males fell to 1.5 per cent— as low as it has ever been in the post-war period—the combined unemployment

15. Unpublished research report prepared for the Manpower Services Commission by the Institute of Manpower Studies, University of Sussex.

rate of youths and women would still be 7.7 per cent[16]. All of this evidence suggests that an expansion of output without special and selective efforts on behalf of these groups will still leave them with unacceptably high rates of unemployment. Consequently, there is an access problem distinct from the level of unemployment and, as mentioned earlier, it is partially related to the fact that if labour is increasingly becoming a fixed factor, enterprises are more conscious about making the investment. Hence, labour force entrants are especially prejudiced, and a broad policy response should include measures that will either increase the enterprise's return on its labour investment, or else reduce the fixed nature of labour as a cost factor.

A major problem associated with the "peripheral" labour force has been raised in relation to its role in maintaining the unemployment gap between aggregate labour demand and supply. If job creation increasingly expands the labour supply by adding peripheral members to the labour force, then the growth process itself must be questioned with regard to its ability to provide paid employment for all who seek it. Several major questions will have to be answered if demand expansion in the medium-term is unable to balance labour demand and supply. Should the economic system, or society, be expected to provide work for everyone who seeks it at prevailing wages? Should priorities be established for the various groups seeking work—for example, should the long-term unemployed have priority over certain new entrants? Should incentives be developed to slow down the rate of entry into the labour force of those now outside it? To what extent should the employment system be made more flexible in order to permit shorter hours of work and job-sharing schemes that will allow a given amount of employment to be spread over a larger number of workers, but with reduced incomes? The foregoing analysis of the labour market provides no answers to these questions, but it does conclude that the potential impact of a continuing influx into the labour force of peripheral workers may require substantial changes in the way the employment system allocates employment opportunities.

The employment problem that is most difficult to come to terms with is that of job content, or job quality, and how this may affect the ability of demand expansion to provide full employment. There is no convincing evidence to suggest that people are becoming more choosy, in fact, in several countries the composition of unemployed has changed more in the direction of job dismissals than to job resignations. On the other hand, it is hard to believe that some of the outward shift of the unemployment-vacancy function is not due to a mismatch between job quality and expectations, and especially so in the light of increasing educational attainments. However, perhaps unemployment is not the variable by which that worker dissatisfaction is expressed. It may be sensed through reduced productivity, increased absenteeism and sick leave, work stoppages, and constant pressure to reduce yearly working hours without a commensurate reduction in income. Consequently, the failure to find a clear relationship between a job-quality/aspiration mismatch and unemployment does not imply that job dissatisfaction does not exist or is not growing and, hence, not an employment problem; it may mean that the dissatisfaction is being otherwise expressed. And if it is being expressed in ways that increase labour costs, then it may indirectly result in unemployment by lowering aggregate labour demand. It is a major employment question that needs further detailed study.

The final employment problem that this analysis dealt with is the measurement of unemployment, and more precisely the usefulness of the aggregate unemployment rate as a guide to policy. One of the obvious shortcomings of the aggregate

16. M. Feldstein, "Lowering the United States Unemployment Rate without Accelerating Inflation", mimeo, 1976.

rate in defining full employment is that it masks quite widespread variations among specific rates by age, sex, occupation, and region, and while these specific rates generally move in the same direction as the aggregate, this is not always the case. Moreover, in some countries the dispersion by age and sex is increasing, which means that the aggregate rate is becoming even less indicative as a general guide to group rates of employment. As was mentioned in the introductory chapter to the present report, the aggregate rate is not a very good indicator of the amount of slack in labour markets either. During economic downturns, much slack is absorbed by reduced working hours, drops in productivity, and withdrawals from the labour force.

The level of the aggregate rate is often associated with different levels of economic hardship; that is, a 7 per cent rate creates more hardship in society than a 5 per cent rate. While an accurate measure of hardship would have to take into account the family incomes of the unemployed, there are three broad indicators that can be monitored to give a slightly more accurate impression of the likely hardship suffered by the unemployed: duration of unemployment, household status of unemployed, and part-time employment[17]. Long-duration unemployment, in most cases, will imply greater economic hardship than a short spell of frictional unemployment. And since duration relative to the aggregate level is increasing slightly in many countries, the aggregate rate may not be a consistent guide—over time and across countries—to hardship. Also, since in the few countries where data were available, it was shown that the percentage of the unemployed who were household heads has fallen, and part-time employment has risen, a given level of unemployment today may overstate economic hardship when compared to past years.

The aggregate rate is often used as an indication of the amount of wage pressure or relief that a change in the level of unemployment will produce. In an important article, Perry has raised the question as to how accurate the aggregate rate was in determining wage pressure in the United States[18]. Very briefly, he concluded that unemployment should be weighted by hours and wages in order to get a more accurate measure of the impact on wages that a changed level of unemployment would produce. The basic assumption, which appears quite realistic, is that it is the full-time, higher-level wage earners who have the greatest impact on wage determination and these tend to be prime-age males. Hence, a preoccupation with the level of unemployment among prime-age males is not an indication that this group is the only concern in implementing full-employment strategies. Rather it means that the level of unemployment of this group is the biggest determinant of the resultant wage pressures likely to follow from a change in the level of employment. Because women and youth and part-time work make up a greater proportion of unemployment today, it takes a correspondingly higher level of unemployment to have the same wage impact than a lower rate had yesterday, when a larger percentage consisted of prime-age males. This approach can explain why an increase in unemployment—the traditional method for bringing down prices—is not as effective today in curbing inflation, since much of the additional unemployment created consists of job seekers (many for the first time), who have little direct impact on wage determination processes. And conversely, it also suggests that selective employment expansion, concentrating primarily on youth and women, would have little impact on inflation.

---

17. For a similar proposal, see Sar A. Levitan and Robert Taggart, *Employment and Earnings Inadequacies: A New Social Indicator*, Baltimore and London, 1974.
18. G. L. Perry, "Changing Labour Markets and Inflation", *Brookings Papers on Economic Activity*, No. 3, 1970, p. 411.

Chart 7

ALTERNATIVE UNEMPLOYMENT RATES

Aggregate unemployment rate
Unemployment rate excluding teenagers
Prime age male (25-54) unemployment rate
Long term unemployment rate
Unemployment rate excluding the under 25 years
Unemployment rate excluding the under 25 years
Prime age males (25-49) unemployment rate

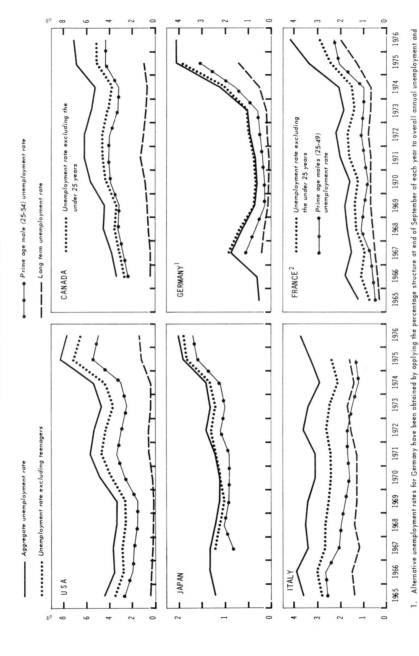

USA

JAPAN

ITALY

CANADA

GERMANY[1]

FRANCE[2]

1. Alternative unemployment rates for Germany have been obtained by applying the percentage structure at end of September of each year to overall annual unemployment and labour force data.
2. March data.

Sources: OECD Labour Force Statistics and National Sources

41

Chart 7 (continued)

ALTERNATIVE UNEMPLOYMENT RATES

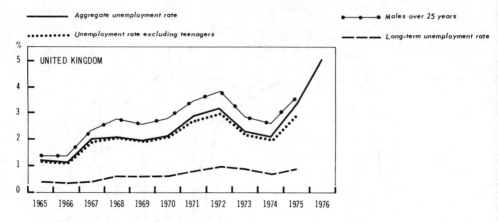

Sources : OECD Labour Force Statistics and National Sources.

Chart 7 illustrates some different measures of unemployment that complement the aggregate rate in directions discussed above. Data limitations prohibit the calculation of part-time and head of household rates, while weighted rates require time-consuming calculations, and the rate excluding teenagers, as well as the prime-age male rate, suggest a first crude approximation of a weighted approach to assess the likely wage impact.

Chapter II

THE CHANGING EMPHASIS OF MANPOWER POLICIES SINCE THE 1960's

SELECTIVE MANPOWER POLICIES UNDER FULL EMPLOYMENT

Since the beginning of the 1960's manpower policies have been developed gradually in the great majority of OECD Member countries. Though the origins of the policy initiative vary between countries, they are all centred around three main objectives:

— to develop human resources and adjust manpower resources to structural changes with a view to fostering *economic growth*;

— to improve the employment opportunities of marginal groups and, thus contribute to *social equity*;

— to improve (in a business-cycle context) the trade-off between *inflation* and *unemployment* by stabilizing employment during the cyclical downswing and by removing labour-market bottlenecks during the upswing.

The first two objectives are primarily of a long-term nature. The equity objective played a major role in North America where economies operated at much higher rates of unemployment compared with Europe. The lower the aggregate rate of unemployment, the better are, of course, the job opportunities for the disadvantaged. It is recalled that in many European countries the situation was characterised by "over-full employment" and perpetual manpower shortages which led to large-scale migratory movements. The growth objective of manpower policies, therefore, was by far the predominant one in Europe.

However, protagonists of an active manpower policy had a more ambitious goal in mind than growth and equity. The long-term and the short-term, they argued, match each other ideally: long-term policies, such as vocational training or rehabilitation, can be speeded up or slowed down according to the conjunctural requirements of the day. For instance, in periods of economic slack, workers, instead of becoming unemployed, can follow training courses and, thus, by acquiring appropriate skills, improve both their individual welfare and the supply conditions for the following upswing. Once the upswing is under way manpower policies continue to fulfil an extremely useful task in that they provide the "head-room" for a smooth expansion of demand and output without inflationary cost pressures by removing potential skill or geographical bottlenecks and by mobilising additional labour force resources. As this was in the golden days of strong growth and steady full employment the latter task received particular attention. In a much-quoted passage of an OECD document this was formulated in the following way: "By promoting the mutual adjustment of

43

manpower needs and resources, an active manpower policy has the special advantage of being expansionist with regard to employment and production, but anti-inflationary with regard to costs and prices"[1]. What was regarded as "special" in these policies was to do with the limitations of demand-management policy. This can only achieve a movement *along* the Phillips curve and thus an uneasy choice between the rate of unemployment and the rate of wage and price inflation has to be made. By contrast, manpower policies were able to shift the Phillips curve *inwards* i.e. to reduce unemployment and inflation simultaneously. The two kinds of policies, however, were not viewed as substitutes for each other but rather as being complementary. The main message was that the results in terms of employment and price stability of any given demand policy stance (be it expansionary or contractive) could be improved by the adoption of selective manpower policies (preferably large-scale).

In the sixties the OECD Manpower and Social Affairs Committee was a major driving force for the promulgation of the concept of an active manpower policy which—albeit closely linked to other policy areas such as social, educational or regional policies—was conceived as a useful complementary tool of general economic management. In 1964 the OECD Council adopted a Recommendation on Manpower Policy as a Means for the Promotion of Economic Growth which urged Member countries to re-examine their manpower policies "with a view to increasing their ability to solve employment problems created by technical and economic change". There were three follow-up reports (1966, 1968 and 1970) on progress made in individual countries in the implementation of the 1964 Recommendation[2]. Simultaneously, detailed country examinations were undertaken under the auspices of the Committee and in close co-operation with the countries concerned. A number of countries have profited from these examinations and their detailed preparation in developing comprehensive new legislation and programmes in the manpower policy field or in reorganising their administrative set-ups for manpower, employment and unemployment benefit services. In many countries, these new initiatives were, in fact, the beginning of an "active manpower policy". Typical examples are: the creation of a new Department of Manpower and Immigration in Canada in 1966, bringing together programmes previously operated by two other Departments and the National Employment Service; the setting up of a new Department of Labour in Ireland in 1966, with particular reference to the need for implementing and active manpower policy; the introduction of new and comprehensive labour-market legislation in Austria (Labour Market Law of 1968) and in Germany (Law on the Promotion of Employment, in 1969).

The 1964 Recommendation was motivated largely by the potential benefits to economic growth of an active manpower policy, i.e. the longer-term objective which is concerned with human-resource development and manpower adaptation to structural change. The short-term objective, of improving the trade-off between full employment and price stability, only gathered some momentum in subsequent years when "creeping" inflation started to affect the OECD area and the Phillips' curve shifted outwards in a number of countries. Before discussing this period, a few observations will be made about the main instruments of an active manpower policy as recognised in the 1964 Recommendation and adopted by a large number of OECD countries.

---

1. *Recommendation of the Council on Manpower Policy as a Means for the Promotion of Economic Growth*, OECD, 1964.
2. *Council report of 25th March, 1966* (unpublished); *Implementation of the OECD Council Recommendation on Active Manpower Policy*, OECD, 1968 ; *Trends and Innovations in Manpower Policy 1967-69*, OECD, 1970.

The OECD Recommendation was *not* limited to labour market policies affecting supply or measures intended to improve the efficiency of employment exchanges with a view to strengthening their clearing-house functions. Equally strong recommendations with regard to the use of selective measures to create employment were also made. But Member governments have, to a larger extent, adopted the first idea of "investment in adaptation" which was the more attractive part of the total manpower policy package, both in terms of political appeal and immediate economic usefulness. Meanwhile, it has become customary in some countries to use the word "manpower policy" as a synonym for those measures affecting labour supply; in other circumstances they are referred to as "traditional manpower measures". In the present report they will be referred to as "manpower adjustment measures" as distinct from "job-creation measures". The term "manpower adjustment" covers measures intended to adapt the pattern of labour supply to a "given" pattern of labour demand (adult training and regional mobility) as well as measures intended to match a "given" pattern of supply to a "given" demand pattern (placement, including all measures to improve job search and job notification). "Job creation" covers all measures designed to increase selectively, i.e., in particular regions or industries or for particular groups of the labour force, or to redistribute, seasonally, the demand for labour. This can be achieved either *directly* through public works projects and public employment, or *indirectly* through financial incentives (tax rebates, loans, or subsidies) to the private sector.

Manpower adjustment policies encompass a wide range of measures which have been enumerated elsewhere[3]. There are two main areas where substantial progress has been made in the last decade or so and one area in which initial expectations have proved to be rather disappointing. Great advances have been made in the area of training and placement measures; efforts to increase geographical mobility, on the other hand, have by and large proven less successful.

The Public Employment Service in many countries was the nucleus and the focal point for the development of an active manpower policy[4]. Such a service was available in most countries and one of the first tasks was to reconsider and possibly redefine its functions in the light of the new manpower policy initiatives. Its two main functions hitherto were to act as a labour exchange and to administer the unemployment insurance system. The labour-exchange function, moreover, was usually restricted to matching job vacancies with—overwhelmingly low-skilled—job seekers. Not surprisingly, the public image was one of an "unemployment office". Given the tight labour markets for skilled and semi-skilled labour, the Public Employment Service was contacted by the most disadvantaged and least-employable groups of the labour force. This in turn, affected its image with employers who lost confidence in the possibility of finding suitable candidates for job openings through the channels of the Public Employment Service.

Great efforts were deployed during the 1960's to improve the placement function. This was in line with the increasing pressures to foster economic growth by a smoothly-functioning labour market which needed ever-increasing transparency, flexibility and speed of response. Typical strategies to achieve this were the extension of vocational counselling and guidance of job seekers; advice on personnel management to private firms; more systematic—albeit less cumbersome—placement through electronic data processing and/or self-service schemes; new training and hiring standards for placement officers, statistical

3. *Ministers of Labour and the Problems of Employment,* Volume I, page 86, OECD, 1976.
4. See Louis Levine, *The Public Employment Service in Social and Economic Policy,* OECD, 1969.

and analytical monitoring of labour market trends; specialised guidance and placement services for marginal groups. The overall aim was to transform the old, negative image of an "unemployment office" into a new, positive image of an "employment service" which would provide to both job seekers and firms a wide range of "services" in the true sense of the word, whilst at the same time being instrumental in implementing a governmental manpower policy. To achieve this end, some countries (Canada, Ireland, United Kingdom) have removed the administration and payment of unemployment insurance from the jurisdiction of the Employment Office. Reorganisation and restructuring along these lines took a long time, but prior to the outbreak of the 1974-75 recession, major progress had been made in many countries, notably in the United Kingdom, France, Germany and Canada.

The introduction of electronic data processing had greatly improved the market transparency and the information flow, which are both vital for an effective and rapid search and placement activity. Pioneer countries in this area were Japan and Belgium, where some clearance was provided for at an inter-regional level, as well as in the United States on a decentralised level ("job banks" for local labour markets). The idea of providing a self-service facility for job seekers without their being registered, including vacancies being advertised by the Employment Service in the mass media originated in Sweden and spread. This procedure provided greater flexibility in the individual's choice (as distinct from computerised matching of demand and supply) and the job seeker could remain anonymous if he so wished. It transpired that this has a considerable attraction to potential job seekers (i.e. not only for those out of work), and contributed to improving the image of the Employment Service. This seemed to be particularly true in the United Kingdom and other countries where the introduction of self-service facilities was part of a wider reshaping of the Employment Service involving the setting up of manpower centres in new premises.

The second major breakthrough in manpower adjustment measures occurred in the field of adult training. Several factors *worked together:* there was the youth education explosion; the increasing social demand for education linked to rising standards of living; rising skill requirements, the obsolescence of certain skills and changing job content in many areas of production affected by rapid technological change; major structural shifts between industrial trades (agriculture, coal mining, the service sector) resulting from economic development or international trade adjustments; new labour-market entrants, such as women and migrants, generally possessing lower vocational skill levels. All these factors contributed to the strong public support of the idea of adult training and the build-up of training facilities. In Europe the existence of tight labour markets created the need to make the workforce occupationally mobile via training and retraining. In North America training was regarded as a major instrument to improve the employability of the hard-to-place unemployed, and this corresponded to the heightened awareness of the problem of poverty, the civil rights movements, and the general effort to achieve a greater degree of equity in society.

The ways and means by which vocational education was handled previously differed considerably; the new structures to be developed for adult training had to be built on these already existing bases. Of necessity, therefore, a certain variety of approaches was adopted in the development of adult training schemes. In Canada, for instance, major emphasis was put on institutional classroom training, whereas the United Kingdom initiated, by way of a levy-grant system, industrial on-the-job training. France introduced a system which placed the main financial burden of adult training on private industry. Germany, which already possessed a rather extensive "dual" system of on-the-job and off-the-job apprenticeship training was able to rely most heavily on retraining and further training programmes in its new active manpower-policy approach. The Swedish model was characterised by a strong emphasis on government training centres which could absorb a large number of applicants at short notice and thus function as a cyclical stabilizer in periods of slackening demand.

These different approaches to the problem make international comparisons of training schemes, both in quantitative and qualitative terms, extremely difficult. Major difficulties also rise from blurred and sometimes questionable distinctions as to general and specific training, youth and adult training or distinctions such as training, retraining, further training, recurrent education, etc. Table 7 is nonetheless an attempt to provide a rough approximation of public expenditure on training schemes in the context of manpower policies.

Table 7. **Expenditure on training schemes as percentage of GNP**

	Fiscal year			Fiscal year	
	1975	1975-1976		1975	1975-1976
Australia		0.11	Netherlands	0.02	
Canada		0.31	New Zealand		0.01
Denmark[1]		0.13	Norway	0.04	
Germany, F.R.	0.27		Sweden[2]		0.34
France[2]	0.19		United Kingdom		0.17
Japan		0.02	United States		0.13

1. Budget figures.
2. As percentage of GDP.

Source: Youth Unemployment, Vol. II, Inventory of measures concerning the employment and unemployment of young people. OECD, in printing.

The rapid expansion of adult training schemes in the late sixties and early seventies did not always yield immediate success. In particular, the earlier phases of habitual generous public spending towards both individuals and employers gave rise to subsequent changes in emphasis and reforms of training policies.

Germany is an illustrative example for the extremely rapid increase in the number of trainees and corresponding public expenditure within a very short time. After the adoption of the Employment Promotion Act in 1969, the number of trainees aided by occupational training-promotion schemes rose from about 50 000 in May 1969 to over 75 000 in mid-1970, and to 140 000 by mid-1971. Expenditure by the Federal Institute of Labour on the promotion of occupational training rose from about DM 300 million in 1969 to about DM 1 500 million in 1971. However, as part of an effort to curb budgetary expenditure, a formerly very generous subsistence allowance paid to trainees has been recently cut back. There is also mounting criticism about the uneven use being made of adult training facilities; those most in need of upgrading their skills have taken least advantage of the new policy measures[5]. In the *United Kingdom* the adoption of the 1964 Industrial Training Act led to rapid expansion of industrial training monitored by Industrial Training Boards and self-financed by a levy-grant system. However, a number of undesirable side-effects occurred, in particular the insufficient integration of industrial training into general manpower policies which led to the Employment and Training Act of 1973. British labour market policy is now administered by the Manpower Service Commission which handles training policies as one element of interrelated policies concerned

5. U. Engelen-Kefer, *Beschäftigungspolitik*, Köln, 1976.

with manpower. The levy-grant system of industrial training has been replaced by a levy-grant-exemption system which gives exemption to small firms and to firms which train their workers adequately. The second major new development is a substantial expansion of retraining and further training under the 1972 Training Opportunities Scheme. In spite of various reforms and the present expansion of training in the United Kingdom, there is concern about the success achieved so far in "raising the quantity of transferable skill training to the level required to meet the needs of industry generally"[6]. The *Canadian* federal manpower training programme was reorganised in 1967 under the Adult Occupational Training Act. Total training expenditure rose from $105 million in 1967-68 to $404 million in 1974-75. In spite of a particularly rapid increase in expenditure on on-the-job training, its share of total expenditure amounted to less than 10 per cent in 1974-75. The strong reliance on institutional classroom training (more than 90 per cent in terms of expenditure) has given rise to criticism. Recently, a Parliamentary Committee recommended "that a substantially increased proportion of total training funds be used to purchase courses for adults to receive skill training in an industrial or working environment because training-in-industry can swiftly be adapted to demands of the labour market[7].

Geographical mobility of labour was given a prominent place in the 1964 Recommendation: conditions should be provided to allow for "a rational reallocation of the labour force". Specific tools suggested were travel and resettlement allowances, housing schemes and provisions to facilitate the social adjustment and integration of people settling in new areas. The underlying philosophy was to encourage manpower movements to areas where job opportunities and growth prospects were good. Most countries have introduced various types of travel, resettlement and removal grants, but on the whole this has not led to as much mobility as was hoped for. Sweden, for instance, had very extensive mobility schemes which achieved some temporary success. But there were several examples of return flows to the original areas. Other countries like Norway and the United Kingdom had depopulated areas which, according to "economic rationality", would become further depopulated, in particular losing working age population as a result of financial aids to mobility. In these countries a strong political opposition to manpower mobility schemes emerged and a clear preference was given to "moving jobs to people" instead of "moving people to jobs". Regional development policies with a strong bias towards stimulating employment opportunities in depressed areas was a widely adopted approach in most countries for removing regional labour-market imbalances.

The need for regional manpower mobility may have been partly overstated. Modern production techniques, notably in the service sector, are geographically less dependent on available resources of primary goods than in earlier phases of industrial development. Another reason, however, may have been the strong influx of foreign workers into expanding countries, which thus did not require a mobile domestic workforce. New inflows of foreign workers were regionally directed to employment demand. Furthermore, the strong job rotation among migrant workers as well as frequent home- and back-flows of migrants between the host countries and the countries of origin provided the means for a smooth and efficient re-allocation of labour in relation to changing industrial and regional manpower requirements. For Germany, for example, this can be confirmed by looking at gross inflows which, between 1962 and 1971, were almost three

6. Department of Employment, *Training for Vital Skills,* London, June 1976.
7. Report of the Standing Senate Committee on National Finance on Canada Manpower, August 1976.

times as high as net inflows (see Table 8). On the other hand, it should be noted that regional mobility measures will again become more relevant once a more buoyant recovery gets under way. This appears even more true for countries which in the past have relied heavily on the recruitment of foreign workers but have discontinued such a policy in the meantime.

Table 8. **F.R. GERMANY**
Migratory flows 1962 to 1971
In millions

Gross inflows	5.16
Backflows	3.22
Net inflows	1.94

Source: Bundesanstalt für Arbeit, *Überlegungen zu einer vorausschauenden Arbeitsmarktpolitik*, Nürnberg, 1974.

The progress made in the field of manpower adjustment measures, in particular training, by far surpassed the development of job-creation programmes. This is at least partly a reflection of the fact that the labour-market situation in the 1960's did not call for employment-creation measures to the same extent as they are required in the mid-1970's. In fact, growth performance being conditioned by supply factors and inflationary pressures originating in manpower shortages, probably meant that insufficient resources were devoted to the supply side of the labour market and that, for a given volume of resources devoted to the policy, more attention was given to the demand side than may have been warranted by the actual situation.

Job creation, in a way, was the older part of the manpower policy package. Several governments had gained experience with "public works" schemes during the Great Depression of the thirties. Under the full-employment conditions of the sixties, the major areas of application were seasonal stabilization and regional development policies and—in particular in the United States—public-works programmes for the disadvantaged. Before returning to some major initiatives taken in this area, it seems worthwhile to mention some particular difficulties in drawing a borderline between "job creation" in a manpower-policy context and in the context of other policy systems. Any policy intervention affecting directly or indirectly the final demand for goods and services has, of course, an indirect effect on employment. In this sense general demand management is to be understood (and since Keynes always has been) as a policy to raise and to stabilize the level of employment, i.e. to create as many jobs are there are job seekers. The only important difference with "job creation" as part of an active manpower policy is its global, i.e. non-selective, nature. It has become common, therefore, to distinguish between the global "big levers" of employment creation via fiscal and monetary policies and selective job stimulation via manpower programmes which are targeted to the particular characteristics of available but unused manpower resources; e.g. hard-to-place workers, surplus labour in less-developed regions, female job-seekers with family responsibilities looking for part-time jobs, etc. This distinction nevertheless remains blurred, in particular in relation to fiscal measures in the form of government purchases or investment programmes. Very often these fiscal programmes are aimed at the employment problems of particular regions or industries and their "selectivity" may thus be particularly strong. The only global measures, in the true sense, are income-tax rebates and regulation of the total money supply[8].

Two main developments in selective employment creation during the sixties are worth mentioning: the United Kingdom regional employment premium and job-creation programmes in the public sector in the United States. The United Kingdom Regional Employment Premium (REP) forms part of a fairly broad package of regional development policies. Introduced in 1967, it provided for the payment of a flat-rate subsidy (differentiated according to sex and youth), for each employed person in manufacturing establishments operating in designated development areas. The REP, thus, discriminates in favour of labour-intensive production (as opposed to capital-intensive production), in favour of operations in development areas (as against the rest of the economy), and in favour of manufacturing (as against services). Discrimination against services was also the objective of an earlier Selective Employment Tax based on the premise that strengthening manufacturing would advance Britain's productivity performance and overall growth rate. The discriminatory effects of the REP against capital investment have to be viewed in the context of the total regional policy package. Most of the other measures, in fact, favour investment activities and the REP can therefore be regarded essentially as redressing the balance between labour and capital incentives. When introduced, the REP was expected to secure a more even distribution of industrial development in Britain by lowering labour costs in Development Areas by 5-10 per cent. Initially intended to be discontinued after seven years of operation, the REP was extended and its size considerably increased after 1974. Total outlays have risen from £103.3 million in 1968-69 (the first full year of REP) to £155.7 million in 1974-75 (this amounted to about half the amount spent in the same year on manpower training). As part of a campaign to consolidate public finance, the scheme was abolished at the beginning of 1977. Evaluations of the effectiveness of the scheme have not been very conclusive, but on the whole they are relatively unfavourable[9].

The second major policy development affecting selectively the demand for labour is illustrated by the United States job-creation programmes. The main objective of these programmes was to raise employment prospects and opportunities for disadvantaged groups, such as blacks, youth, immigrants and inner-city populations. Unlike the prevailing situation in Europe, the challenge in the United States was not to tap potential manpower resources to foster growth, but rather to provide jobs for those in need, in order to promote equality. The emergence and persistence of disadvantaged minorities in an otherwise prosperous society gave rise to considerable concern, analysis and a trial-and-error approach towards a great variety of policy measures. The employment problem is but one dimension—albeit an essential one—of the total problem, other dimensions being poverty and discrimination. Job-creation measures had to be closely linked with action in these other areas.

The United States experience with job-creation measures is characterised by a multitude of relatively small and often short-lived programmes and, over the years, a rising need for better co-ordination and cohesion of these programmes. Detailed surveys of the different programmes are abundant[10]. The following is

---

8. For a fuller treatment of the interfaces of manpower policies with other policy areas, see R.A. Jenness, *Manpower and Employment Problems and Prospects,* OECD, forthcoming. A systematic review of the effects and costs of alternative fiscal policies on the level of employment will be provided in Chapter III of the present report.

9. For a review see P.S. Hare, *The Principles and Uses of Regional Employment Subsidies,* The Institute for Fiscal Studies, 1976.

10. For instance: D. Werneke, "Job Creation Programmes: The United States Experience", *International Labour Review,* Vol. 114, No. 1, July-August 1976, p. 43.

a very rough guide to the main features. Two major pieces of legislation, the Manpower Development and Training Act of 1962 and the Employment Opportunity Act of 1966 provided the legal basis of and funding for the earlier manpower programmes. The biggest and best-known programmes were *Neighbourhood Youth Corps,* providing young people from poor families with temporary jobs in special work projects (mostly in local community services); *Operation Mainstream,* focusing on chronically-unemployed adults; *New Careers,* providing "subprofessional" entry jobs, mostly in the public sector; *Job Opportunities in the Business Sector,* which was the only major programme for job-creation in the private sector. These programmes had in common their selectivity with regard to special groups in the labour force, suffering from one or more employability handicaps. Secondly, all these programmes were founded and administered centrally by the Federal Government. The Employment Emergency Act of 1971, responding to the cyclical downturn of employment, introduced a new type of programme: the *Public Employment Programme* was intended to absorb unemployment resulting from the recession. The programme gave priority to designated target groups but was not limited to the disadvantaged. It was also applied in regional areas where unemployment exceeded the national average. Local authorities in these areas received federal funds for transitional hiring of public employees for up to two years. But the actual stay of an individual in a PEP job was on average much less than two years. In 1973 the total manpower policy concept of the United States was redesigned under the Comprehensive Employment and Training Act which replaced the previous manpower legislation and programmes. The aim of this new act was both to consolidate and to decentralise the large number of individual programmes. The Act laid emphasis on the dual objectives of reducing aggregate unemployment and raising the employability of the disadvantaged. Job creation and measures to increase the productivity of the disadvantaged (notably training) were regarded as equally important. However, due to the recession, job-creation's share of total funding, in particular for public sector employment, has received the major emphasis in subsequent years.

THE WORSENING TRADE-OFF BETWEEN UNEMPLOYMENT AND INFLATION

Having discussed a number of major breakthroughs in specific manpower measures, both those affecting the supply and those affecting the demand side of the labour market in selected OECD countries, we shall now return to the shifting emphasis of the total manpower package prior to the 1974-75 recession. Taking the above-mentioned OECD reports on the implementation of the 1964 Recommendation as a framework, a clear trend emerges of laying more emphasis on the short-term objective of active manpower policy, i.e. that of maintaining high levels of employment over the business cycle period while at the same time combating inflation. In many OECD countries during the late sixties, "creeping" inflation gave rise to serious concern on the part of policy-makers. The need for developing comprehensive anti-inflationary strategies was stressed in a major OECD report in 1970, in which prominent place was given to selective manpower measures[11]. Great efforts were made to convince governments that by resorting to selective action they might be able to avoid stop-go policies to which otherwise they were committed due to successive recessionary and inflationary cycles. The Manpower and Social Affairs Committee repeatedly

11. *Inflation, The Present Problem,* OECD, 1970.

urged closer integration and better tuning of demand management and active manpower policies. The following quotation provides a typical example: "Any move towards economic restraint for the sake of disinflation, which can be expected to create unemployment, should be combined *from the outset* with preparation of selective counter-action. Similarly, any policy move towards overall expansion through general demand management should be combined with measures to facilitate and stimulate appropriate reallocation of resources so as to avoid the emergence of inflationary shortages"[12].

There can be no doubt that this part of the concept of an active manpower policy met with considerable scepticism and in the end gained much less ground in actual policy-making than the original long-term manpower development objectives of active manpower policy. The only noteworthy exception is Sweden, where emergency programmes and quick-acting responses to labour market policies have been used as an important counter-cyclical (as well as anti-inflationary) weapon[13]. In early 1967, employment prospects for the Swedish economy deteriorated rapidly as a result of a downturn in world demand. Reflationary action by global fiscal-monetary policies was rejected on the grounds of inflationary pressures and a weak balance-of-payments position. There was a considerable dispersion in unemployment rates between industries and regions; general reflationary measures would have created supply bottlenecks in those areas and industries which were still in a relatively tight labour-market situation; such measures probably would have been insufficient to alleviate the unemployment situation in other areas and industries. Against this background the government developed a short-term selective manpower strategy based mainly on job creation and retraining. The following table gives an indication of the order of magnitude of the numbers of people affected by these measures, as well as the speed of implementation. The speed is particularly striking with respect to training measures which, under normal circumstances, require a considerable lead-time for the development of adequate structures, programmes and facilities. However, Sweden had, in previous years, undertaken a major effort to build up these training structures with the explicit intention of using them at short notice in response to cyclical labour-market developments. The cyclical employment trend was reversed in 1968, but this was first accompanied by a return of discouraged workers to the labour market. The short-term employment measures were therefore maintained for some months, but after March 1969 selective employment-creation measures were phased out rapidly and the emphasis of training activities was shifted towards disadvantaged groups.

Table 9. **SWEDEN**
**Persons affected by short-term employment measures
as a percentage of total labour force**

	Total	of which: Retraining
March 1966	1.1	0.6
March 1967	1.6	0.7
March 1968	2.6	0.9

Source: *Adult training as an instrument of active manpower policy*, OECD, 1972.

12. *Trends and Innovations in Manpower Policy, 1967-69*, OECD, 1970.
13. See: *Adult Training as an Instrument of Active Manpower Policy*, OECD, 1972.

The idea of using manpower policies as a counter-cyclical weapon gained some ground in a few other countries during the 1967 recession. But the interest in government circles was often restricted to the idea of keeping dismissed labour out of the unemployment register by putting it onto training. In order to achieve this it was necessary to develop adequate training structures and facilities. During these years, it was suggested as a target that a country should be in the position, i.e. possess the necessary training institutions, the personnel and training programmes, to absorb, at short notice, at least 1 per cent of the labour force which otherwise would become idle as a result of slackening economic activities. Only Sweden and Canada come near to this target figure. Yet only in Sweden, but not in Canada, was the expansion of adult training operated mainly as a counter-cyclical device.

The limited success of the short-term anti-cyclical concept of manpower policy was due to many reasons. To use training programmes according to the conjonctural requirements of the day was regarded by many, and notably edu-cationalists, as a frivolous way of responding to the social demand for education. It has turned out to be extremely difficult, even in the short term, to forecast skill requirements and, thus, to design training programmes which responded directly to the future needs of the economy. Short-term training courses are often insufficient for the bulk of unskilled workers to raise their skill level or to retrain workers whose skills have become obsolete. On the institutional side, both for job-creation and training measures, there were simply too many lags to make possible the rapid shifts of methods and resources that are necessary if the policy is to play a conjonctural stabilization role. Many policy-makers regarded the tools of demand management as sufficient to achieve reasonable stabilization of cyclical swings in output and employment. Moreover, the claimed anti-inflationary thrust of manpower policies was not felt to be credible, notably because there was little evidence that substantial inflationary pressures actually originated in manpower bottlenecks. But given the relatively modest scale of manpower programmes actually implemented in most countries, their potential counter-inflationary impact remains to be tested.

The scope and role of manpower policies prior to the outbreak of the recession have been analysed already in this chapter. The next section will deal with the changing emphasis of active manpower policies during the recession. Before moving on it might be useful to *summarise* the main points made so far. The 1964 Recommendation of the OECD Manpower and Social Affairs Committee prepared the ground for the adoption of the concept as well as the actual implementation of an active manpower policy in many OECD countries. Governments increasingly appreciated the potential benefits of an active manpower policy with regard to human resource development, mobilisation of untapped manpower resources, facilities for adjustment to economic and technological change and providing job opportunities for the disadvantaged. What convinced policy-makers was thus the potential role of an active manpower policy in contributing to economic growth and equality of opportunity. In line with this, the most spectacular advances occurred in adult training and the improvement of the placement service. Initially high expectations with regard to stimulating geograph-ical mobility were not fulfilled. The creation of jobs in particular regions and industries and for particular groups of the labour force, i.e., selective stimul-ation of the demand for labour, was in many countries a well-established policy tool. Nevertheless, new initiatives were also taken in this area, such as the Regional Employment Premium in the United Kingdom and public and private employment programmes for disadvantaged workers in the United States. The increasing concern with "creeping" inflation since the late sixties and the persis-tent deterioration of the trade-off between inflation and unemployment lead many policy advisers (including the OECD) to stress the potential role of an active manpower policy in mitigating the unemployment-inflation dilemma. In order to fulfil this role, the necessary machinery for rapid action in the labour market and a careful co-ordination of general-demand management and selective-manpower policies is required. With the noteworthy exception of Sweden, these ideas did not gain much ground in actual policy-making.

EMPLOYMENT AND MANPOWER POLICIES DURING THE RECESSION

The upsurge of food and world commodity prices in 1973 prompted restrictive government action towards the expansion of aggregate demand which was strengthened in 1974 in order to mitigate the inflationary effects of the oil crisis. This, occurring concurrently with a number of other adverse developments such as running down stocks of finished goods and the cumulative effect of simultaneously regressing world trade in all major industrial countries, lead to the most severe recession since the thirties. Some improvement in business climate has occurred since the later part of 1975, resulting in a gradual resumption of output growth in some important OECD countries (notably the United States, Japan and Germany). The much-expected economic recovery, however, was frequently interrupted by a number of setbacks. The OECD area, so far, has not regained a state of self-sustained expansion and the outlook is clouded by uncertainties.

A detailed survey of measures taken during the 1974-75 recession was undertaken in preparation for the 1976 Meeting of the Manpower and Social Affairs Committee at Ministerial level[14]. The results of this survey have been reviewed and analysed in great detail for the Ministerial Meeting[15]. There is therefore no need to repeat the information and arguments available elsewhere. A brief overview of what appear to be the main innovations and changes of emphasis in the pursuit of active manpower policies during the recession may however make it possible to separate the relevant from the less relevant factors and thus provide a useful platform from which future manpower policy trends can be judged.

The main policy line adopted by the majority of countries facing declining demand and output was to encourage the maintenance of existing employment as much and as long as possible, and—to the extent that this failed—to maintain the income of those who became unemployed. One method not adopted as a major strategy was any effort to counteract declining employment by creating new employment. The basic attitude was thus defensive, characterised by the intention to cushion the individual from the economic hardships of the recession.

However, a few countries adopted strong counter-cyclical demand policies aimed at weak labour markets. Sweden, in particular, made use of special investment funds to stabilize investment activity. In addition, assistance in stockpiling was given to firms facing difficulties in selling manufactured goods. On condition that workers were not dismissed, these firms received a government grant amounting to 20 per cent of the value of the increase in stocks above a "normal" level at a base period. During 1975 and 1976, 1 500 firms were granted stockpiling

14. An updated version of this survey will be available shortly under the title "Inventory of Employment and Manpower Measures" (mimeographed).

15. *Ministers of Labour and the Problems of Employment*, Vols. I and II, OECD, 1976 and 1977.

assistance, representing one-third of total industrial employment. It has been estimated that the wage costs of the workers retained have been reduced by about 50 per cent as a result of the subsidy[16].

Table 10. **Expenditure on temporary employment maintenance or creation as percentage of GNP**

	Fiscal year			Fiscal year	
	1975	1975-1976		1975	1975-1976
Australia		0.18	Netherlands	0.35	
Canada		0.10	New Zealand		0.10
Denmark[1]		1.28	Norway	0.14	
Germany, F.R.	0.35		Sweden[2]		0.88
France[2]	0.04		United Kingdom		0.22
Japan		0.01	United States		0.30

1. Budget figures.
2. In per cent of GDP.

Source: Youth Unemployment, Vol II, Inventory of measures concerning the employment and unemployment of young people. OECD, in printing.

Stabilization of the demand for goods and services and thereby employment was successful only in a few of the smaller OECD countries (Sweden, Norway, Austria). The great majority of countries was drawn into the wake of the world recession. In Europe and Japan the main policy response in the employment area was to maintain existing jobs as long as possible in spite of declining demand and output. This strategy, which in Sweden is labelled "the first line of defence", gives priority to safeguarding jobs in individual firms as distinct from measures to re-employ those having lost their jobs through some form of government assistance. The basic intention is, in the context of a severe recession, to maintain workers' job attachment and to avoid the slow but steady deterioration of their employability usually associated with the unemployment experience. Several European countries gave financial assistance to weak firms or sectors in order to maintain the latters' liquidity position and to ensure their survival. Other countries introduced (by law or collective agreements) provisions which made dismissals, in particular of older workers, very costly or difficult. The most original protective device was the large-scale subsidising of existing jobs by paying benefits either to workers who were compelled—whilst staying in their jobs—to work fewer than the standard number of hours per week, or to employers who refrained from resorting to otherwise necessary dismissals[17].

Income-maintenance policy was the most vigorously and uniformly adopted approach in the OECD area. In several countries the coverage and duration, as well as the administrative set-up of unemployment compensation systems had been improved and extended just prior to the outbreak of the recession. Due to the automaticity of these systems rising unemployment triggered off a substantial

16. G. Rehn, "Needs and Methods for Further Development of Manpower Policy", mimeo., 1976.
17. For a detailed comparative review of job security measures adopted by governments as well as labour and management in the United Kingdom, Germany and France during the recent recession, see John Gennard, *Job Security and Industrial Relations,* OECD, forthcoming. This report estimates that "in the United Kingdom, had the Government not introduced policies of selective financial assistance and financial incentives to employers not to declare workers redundant, then unemployment would have been 500 000 more than it otherwise was. A large proportion of this is accounted for by the estimated savings from the rescue of British Leyland and Chrysler".

increase of public expenditure for unemployment compensation. During the recession the coverage and duration was further extended in several countries.

Both manpower-adjustment and selective job-creation measures had to be operated within the constraints of tight budgets and deflationary demand policies. As there is no automatic trigger comparable to unemployment compensation payments, manpower-policy measures have to compete with other public expenditure and the time lags between rising unemployment, public concern and public support tend to be unduly long. The existence of generous unemployment compensation makes these time lags even longer. For these reasons it has been suggested that expenditure on active manpower measures be linked to unemployment levels and to let these measures, rather than income maintenance payments, play the role of an automatic stabilizer throughout the business cycle[18]. Others have suggested channelling unemployment compensation expenditure, triggered off as a result of high unemployment, into job-creation schemes, provided the cyclical downswing turns out to be a prolonged one. The underlying philosophy of these proposals is that paying people for working or for being trained should always be chosen in preference to paying them for prolonged and involuntary inactivity. However, no country so far has adopted a radical and consequent switch from a defensive policy of income protection to an aggressive approach to job creation[19].

It must be borne in mind that those areas of active manpower policies where the most spectacular advances had occurred in the past, i.e. manpower training and placement schemes, could contribute relatively little to reducing the jobless rate. To enrol the unemployed in government-sponsored training courses could be a partial solution for a limited number of people but not for the bulk of job seekers suddenly flooding the market. Nevertheless, a most original and quantitatively relevant device, consisting of combining job attachment, job preservation in the private sector and on-the-job training was used by Sweden. A flat-rate training subsidy (amounting to 20-65 per cent of average wage costs in industry) was given to employers who abstained from laying off employees in connection with cutbacks in production, and who instead provided training. By April 1977, one per cent of Sweden's total work force was involved in this programme.

The role of placement services was even less relevant than training schemes in contributing to an improvement in the employment situation. The unemployment problem, essentially, did not result from a mismatch between demand and supply patterns, which could have been overcome by more market transparency and labour flexibility. There was an aggregate demand deficit for labour characterised by the number of job seekers outstripping a very small number of vacancies. Moreover, placement services are only able to deal with some specific kinds of mismatch unemployment, e.g. the regional and industrial dispersion of job-seekers and job opportunities. They can only contribute to counteracting occupational imbalances to a lesser extent, and then only in conjunction with training schemes. To judge from regional, industrial and occupational differences between unemployment rates, there is no evidence that the dispersion, and thus the likelihood of a mismatch between supply and demand patterns has increased during the recent recession. On the other hand, the possibility that imbalances have arisen because of strong compositional changes on the supply side and in particular the age and sex structure of the labour force cannot be excluded. It is

18. The USA is actively considering a stand-by, triggered counter-cyclical public service employment programme.
19. Though it must be borne in mind that Sweden had adopted an offensive approach initially, namely, the "first line of defence" idea mentioned earlier.

frequently argued, for instance, that high rates of youth unemployment caused by relatively high starting wages are currently a most significant form of market distortion. Be that as it may, it is significant to note that placement measures are not able to deal with this kind of mismatch.

Selective job creation appears to be the most potentially effective weapon for protecting the labour market against the adverse effects of a recessive downturn of demand and output. But in spite of a wide range of possible lines of action there is no particular measure which, as such and by itself, would provide an ideal solution[20]. Public works, i.e., special public-investment programmes (mainly contracted to private construction firms) which had been used on a large scale in the thirties, are now considered to be not selective enough to last too long and to be difficult to initiate, and too difficult to phase out when the general economic climate improves, and too capital- and skill-intensive they are, in short, expected to feed inflation and thus be counter-productive in the present economic context. The extension of public-sector employment as an instrument of policy may be conceived either in the form of accelerated recruitment in areas such as health, education, social security, etc., or in the form of special government programmes intended to offer new kinds of public services. The first approach, i.e. boosting the manning of existing government services, is currently unpopular in a number of countries. The government sector has greatly expanded over the last decade and, it is argued, has over-strained productive resources, thus contributing to inflation. There is considerable public pressure against increasing bureaucratic structures and "big government". The second approach, that of drawing up special government programmes to occupy the unemployed, has been criticised as a "make-work" arrangement with little productive value. During the recession however, some innovative and socially-useful public programmes have been implemented in a few countries and this seems promising for new and positive developments. The basic idea is to provide financial aid to voluntary agencies and local communities which then develop and administer programmes on their own initiative. Such decentralised programmes are able to respond to immediate social needs in a quick and unbureactic fashion. Typical examples are the Local Initiative Programme of Canada, the Community Industry Scheme of the United Kingdom and the Youth Training Programme of Ireland[21].

The crucial challenge, according to many, is not creating jobs in the public sector but expanding employment in the private sector. If, however, the aggregate level of demand for goods and services continues to be held back for anti-inflationary reasons, it is extremely difficult to induce firms to hire workers. In particular, in a growth economy, private firms tend to make investment and recruitment decisions overwhelmingly on the basis of expectations about the economic climate in general and their sales prospects in particular. There are two possible ways to stimulate private recruitment on a selective basis; to strengthen the demand for goods and services selectively (for instance, by reducing the sales tax on passenger vehicles) or by subsidising production costs, and in particular, labour costs. The latter approach has been the one used by several countries during the recent recession[22].

The Meeting of Labour Ministers in March 1976 re-affirmed the commitment of OECD governments to full employment, subject to a progressive reduction

---

20. The following chapter will deal in some detail with a number of selective measures to raise the demand for labour.
21. Another example is the current "projects" approach under the United States public service employment programme, under which funds are only released for specified decentralised projects (as distinct from regular public-service jobs).
22. This will be further analysed in the following chapter.

of inflation. Ministers reviewed current manpower policies and attempted to reactivate the policy concept by enlarging its field of application. They conceived of a "general employment and manpower policy" which should be integrated into the framework of economic policies on the one hand and social policies on the other. In order to expand employment, a better balance between income maintenance and positive manpower utilisation should be achieved. Stimulation of employment, manpower adaptation, and equality of employment opportunities are all important, and require further development. International co-operation in the employment area and co-operation with employers and unions are becoming increasingly and urgently necessary.

Although the discussions at the Ministerial meeting reflected concern about the likely gap—both for short-term and structural reasons—between the development of output and the reduction of unemployment, the general attitude was one of moderate optimism as to the capacity of policy measures to overcome the employment crisis in the not-too-distant future. This optimism meanwhile has now cooled off considerably due to the hesitancy and weakness of the upturn in the OECD area as a whole. Day-to-day policy-making, therefore, faces a serious dilemma since the great majority of employment and manpower measures adopted during the recession were based on the assumption that a cyclical upturn would occur at an opportune moment.

Chapter III

POLICIES TO RAISE THE DEMAND FOR LABOUR

The current discussion of manpower policies in relation to the full-employment objective tends to neglect the fact that in the past these policies were mainly designed to operate in a full employment context, i.e., to promote economic growth, equity, and—in some countries—to diminish inflationary pressures through manpower adaptation and development policies. The main exception was regional employment-creation policies designed to redistribute employment creation spatially within the context of an overall expansion of output and employment, or to stabilize employment over a seasonal or short cyclical downswing. The seriousness of the recession and the outlook for continuing under-utilisation of manpower resources related to a number of non-cyclical forces, such as demographic supply profiles, growing female participation in the labour force and, possibly, declining investment opportunities, may well require a reorientation and new emphasis of manpower policy as compared with its present scope and direction.

Against this background, it appears useful to clarify the potential role of selective employment policies within a more general full-employment strategy by analysing the impact of alternative ways of creating employment. This is the essential purpose of the present chapter. It will assess selective manpower measures (basically, employment subsidies to private industry and direct job creation in the public sector) on a comparative basis with global employment-stimulating measures (basically taxation and non-selective expenditure). The various global and selective measures will be analysed sequentially in relation to cost effectiveness, effects on inflation and other criteria. This will provide a basis for consideration of the total profile of a policy package to raise the demand for labour consisting of a mix of global demand management and selective measures.

The desired level of employment is only one of a number of policy objectives which traditionally are pursued concurrently by government economic policy-makers. Other major considerations include the state of public sector financial balances, the rate of inflation and the balance of payments. In view of such considerations, it follows that alternative measures to raise the demand for labour need to be assessed according to criteria such as the extent to which they bring about a net increase in employment, the net financial cost per additional job, the value of the extra output, how quickly the measure takes effect, how quickly it can be phased out, its effect on inflation, on the balance of payments, on industrial recovery, and the extent to which measures can be "targeted" at particular categories of the unemployed. In respect of each of these criteria the time-scale of the build-up of the effects is often important because in comparing

59

alternative policies it is important to know whether, for example, one policy has greater short-run effects, thereby making their relative cost effectiveness vary with the given time horizon. These criteria are largely *internal* with respect to any given Member country. But another important consideration must be their implications for the *rest of the OECD countries,* e.g. tax cuts help to raise the employment level in other countries by raising demand for their exports whereas wage subsidies could have the opposite effect.

Clearly countries differ in terms of their overall economic policies and the constraints which affect them, but a number of broad generalisations are nonetheless possible. If, in a particular country, no further reflationary action is contemplated, whether through fear of exacerbating inflation, the balance-of-payments deficit or the public sector financial deficit[1], it is necessary to consider whether, through a new mixture of policy measures, employment might nevertheless be increased or prevented from falling further. For example, if the cost per job of one policy measure is lower than in the case of another policy, employment can be increased without increasing the financial deficit by expanding the former programme at the expense of the latter. Given this sort of possibility it follows that another country reducing its financial deficit by cutting total expenditure or raising total taxation, might nonetheless avoid, or at least minimise, the reduction in employment by raising the relative share in total expenditure of measures with the lowest cost-per-job. Alternatively, if the reflation of overall economic activity is being considered it is necessary to consider whether suitably selective policies exist which have a larger/faster impact on employment than others with the same financial costs. Of course, if such possibilities exist it still remains necessary, as was made clear earlier, to consider their implications for inflation, the balance of payments and economic efficiency.

TAXATION AND NON-SELECTIVE EXPENDITURE MEASURES

Taxation

A basic feature of tax cuts of all kinds is that they raise employment by first raising aggregate demand then, in consequence, output (and imports) and, after a further time-lag, employment. Under certain circumstances, however, employment will be increased in anticipation of the expected rise in output induced by a tax cut. Tax cuts produce a loss of revenue, but as demand and employment rise this will be offset partly by the return flow via increased indirect tax revenue in respect of increased sales of goods and services, increased income tax and social security contributions as a result of increased employment, and a reduction in expenditure on unemployment-related benefits. The effect on employment will normally build up only after a time-lag, but will continue to grow thereafter, provided the reduced revenue is not matched by reduced expenditure.

A cut in *income tax* will have the above general features in addition to which it will have no impact on the relative prices of goods produced domestically either vis-à-vis one another, or in respect of the prices of imports, except insofar as wage claims are moderated in which case (given the exchange rate) competitiveness and the real balance of trade will improve[2]. A reduction in *indirect* taxes will reduce the growth of prices and in consequence wages and domestic

1. Leaving aside the question of a causal relationship between the PSD and inflation.
2. These assumptions underlie the estimates for income tax cuts shown in Tables 11, 12 and 13.

costs, so that there will be a reduction in the price of domestic goods relative to foreign goods (at a given exchange rate), apart from which the effects will be broadly similar to those induced by increased income taxation.

A reduction in *corporate profits* tax might, in the short term, be divided between increased retained profits (savings), increased dividends, lower prices and increased investment—all but the first will eventually induce some increased demand, output and hence employment. However, the relative financial importance of each such effect and their precise implications for demand and employment are subject to considerable differences of assessment depending on the precise circumstances in which the tax cut is introduced; in any case, cuts in corporation tax are ineffective in conditions (e.g. the United Kingdom and the Netherlands) where taxable profits have almost vanished anyway.

A reduction in *employer's social security contributions* is probably also a relatively uncertain way of reflating output and employment in the short-term. The effect on demand would be slow to build up and would occur after a time-lag in response to the reduction in prices (or rate of growth of prices) associated with the reduction in manpower costs implied by lower contributions; but the transformation into lower prices of reduced contributions itself would be subject to time-lags, while the demand-output-employment reactions would involve further lags so that the effect on employment would be long delayed. There would be a separate longer-run effect via the structure of the relative prices of labour and capital—labour becoming relatively cheaper and hence more attractive—except insofar as the current incidence of employers' contributions falls on wages, i.e., if wages are lower now than they otherwise would be with lower contributions, all that would happen would be a change in the split of labour costs between wages and contributions—the former increasing in response to a cut in the latter. In other words, the short-run employment effects are smaller than an income tax cut costing the same amount and the longer-run response in terms of employment is more conjectural. (This is not to say that a massive cut in employers' contributions would not produce a greater effect, but it would cost more than an income tax cut with the same employment effect; further, if its impact on the finances of social security schemes were offset by an increase in *employees'* contributions, the net effect would be deflationary because the reduction in demand per unit of employees' increased contributions would exceed the increase in demand per unit of employers' contributions.)

In brief, in the case of taxation, the most certain and largest impact on employment in the short term for a given financial cost is likely to be obtained from "general" reflationary measures such as cuts in income or consumption taxes rather than those which perhaps seem, at first sight, to be more directly related to profits and industrial costs.

However, even in the case of cuts in income or indirect tax, the employment effects are likely to be relatively low by comparison with other possible measures in the field of public expenditure. Tax cuts raise real personal disposable income in response to which consumption will rise, though with a time-lag. Estimates of the consumption response vary[3], but it might take in the region of two years before consumption has adjusted fully to the tax cut. In the meantime, there is a leakage into savings which does not raise demand, output and employment. As for the fraction of the expenditure which raises demand, it takes time for output and then employment to respond. The significance of this point will emerge more clearly when public expenditure and *a fortiori* selective-employment measures are considered below.

---

3. Estimates vary both within a given country according to the estimation model used, and between countries.

Non-selective public expenditure measures

Countries clearly vary in the extent to which they feel that the total of public expenditure can absorb an increased share of national economic resources. It is not the present intention to comment on that issue, except to note that a growing number of countries appears to feel that the public sector share has reached its tolerable limit (whether because of short-run concern with the size of the budget deficit or the longer-run implications for tax burdens). This means in practice that it is unlikely that, to extent that any further reflationary action is taken, increases in the total of public expenditure will play a major role. Nonetheless, it is necessary to consider the employment effects of different types of public expenditure within a given total.

The greatest impact on employment would arise if the government were simply to *increase the size of its own labour force,* spending the entire amount of any additional expenditure on manpower in existing public-expenditure programmes. For example, it could increase the size of the armed forces, or it could increase staffing ratios in schools, hospitals, etc. Subject to the availability of suitably qualified labour and complementary physical equipment and buildings this would be the largest and fastest way of raising employment. It would, however, imply a substantial shift in the public-sector share of the labour force which in some countries would run counter to current policies and which would be difficult to reverse later.

Table 11. UNITED KINGDOM
Effects of £400 million (per year) tax cuts
and increased expenditure, after 2 years

	Employ-ment 000's	Net cost to the exchequer	Net cost per job £ per week
Income tax	40	320	150
Current grants	55	300	100
Current expenditure on goods and services	130	200	30

Source: Secretariat estimates based on H.P. Evans and C.J. Riley, *Simulations with the Treasury Model,* H.M.S.O., 1974.

Table 12. UNITED STATES
Effects of programmes costing $1 billion

	Year 1			Year 2		
	Employ-ment 000's	Net cost to the government $ Mill.	Net cost per job $ per week	Employ-ment 000's	Net cost $ Mill.	Net cost per job $ per week
Income tax cut	10	650	1 150	30	650	390
Government purchase	20	650	600	50	650	255
Public service employment	80	440	110	70	370	100
Public works[1]	15	480	660	35	500	265

1. Economic Development Administration.

Source: OECD Secretariat estimates, based on the following Congressional Budget Office publications: *Short-Run Measures to Stimulate the Economy,* March 1977; *The Disappointing Recovery,* January 1977; *The Economic Outlook,* February 1978.

Table 13. CANADA
Effect of a $500 million change in expenditure on employment
Percentage increase in total employment

	4th quarter	8th quarter
Income tax	0.27%	0.51%
Transfers	0.21%	0.44%
Current expenditure on goods and services	0.43%	0.60%

Source: Cook, Jump, Hodgins, Szabo, *Economic Impact of Selected Government Programmes directed towards the Labour Market,* Economic Council of Canada, 1976.

After increases in the manpower content of existing programmes the largest employment effect for a given outlay could be achieved by an increase in *current public expenditure on goods and services* at existing staffing ratios. Perhaps on average about two-thirds of the amount spent will directly represent increased employment incomes as soon as the funds are spent. The effect on employment will grow further with the passage of time via the dynamic reactions of income, demand and output in the economy generally. The increase in employment will mean that the *net* cost of this measure will be below the initial gross expenditure as a result of reduced expenditure on unemployment benefits and increased revenue from taxation. This route will create more jobs than reductions in income or indirect taxation and will work more quickly because the increase in demand is simultaneous with the outlay (unlike a tax cut there is no direct leakage into personal savings and only a small leakage into indirect taxation). The balance-of-payments effect might be larger than in the case of a tax cut although this depends on whether or not the greater impact on demand of increased public expenditure is offset by the greater import content of increased private sector demand induced by tax cuts. Unlike indirect tax cuts there will be no reduction in the rate of inflation.

An increase in expenditure on public sector *capital* projects (roads, housing) often has the character of being selective in relation to employment creation and is discussed below under selective measures.

In the case of *transfer payments* to lower income households (pensions, etc.) the impact on employment works in the same way as a tax cut, running from the initial increase in disposable income through increased demand then output to higher employment. But as the leakage into savings is likely to be weaker than in the case of a tax cut[4], the speed with which demand reacts to the increase in disposable income and the eventual size of the reactions means that the employment effect will be both faster and larger than in the case of a tax cut. The effect might, however, be smaller than in the case of increased public spending on goods and services. Unlike a cut in indirect taxes there will be no reduction in the rate of inflation, except insofar as unions accept lower wage settlements than otherwise would have been the case in response to increased transfer payments; on the other hand, in some countries there is growing opposition on the part of those in work to greater cash benefits for those who do not work. It is also possible, but by no means certain, that improved transfers to those not in work would provide an incentive to those in work to cease employment, at least temporarily. On the other hand, if the transfer payments were for workers as well as others (e.g. child allowances) the latter problem need not

---

4. i.e. the propensity to spend of lower-income households is greater than in the case of income-tax payers or the population generally.

arise, but then the demand (and hence employment) effect need not be significantly larger than in the case of a tax cut. The balance-of-payments cost is likely to be larger than in the case of a tax cut (insofar as the demand effect is also greater); by comparison with public expenditure on goods and services the difference is uncertain because on the one hand the import content of the demand induced by increased cash transfers will be greater, but on the other hand the total increased demand induced by transfers might, in the short run, be smaller because of savings. A complication which arises with transfer payments, but not other public spending, is that insofar as specific social security funds are involved, increased spending would create (or increase) financial deficits; if this were offset by increased contributions or tax-financed Treasury subsidies the net increase in demand and employment would depend upon whether or not the transfers went to the poorest and those not in work, such as the elderly, or to workers generally (in which case the net effect could be negligible or nil).

Summary: Taxes and non-selective expenditure measures

Tables 11, 12 and 13 illustrate the above arguments.

The strongest short-run *employment* effects are probably via current public expenditure on employment, current public expenditure on goods and services, and cash transfers in that order (although, depending on the extent of prior planning, and the capital/labour ratios, capital projects could be fairly cost-effective), followed by income or indirect tax cuts; *costs-per-job* (whether measured gross or after increases in tax revenue and reductions in unemployment benefits) will necessarily vary with the employment effect.

Turning to the rate of *inflation,* the strongest effect in terms of reduction is via reduced indirect tax cuts; reductions in employers' social security contributions or other payroll taxes will have a weaker effect (and one which will be slow to build up); it is conceivable that cuts in income tax or increased transfer payments might have a favourable impact if they induced unions to accept lower wage settlements, otherwise they might rather tend to stimulate inflation. These effects are separate from and additional to any effects of a "Phillips curve" nature, which will vary with the employment effect of each measure.

The *balance-of-payments* effects are the most uncertain and difficult to establish. They depend on four separable factors:

i)   the increase in total demand;
ii) the import content of that demand;
iii) any changes in competitiveness induced by the measures; and
iv) the response of trade volumes to any such change in competitiveness. The increase in total demand associated with each measure is broadly indicated by their relative employment effects (i.e. higher for public expenditure than for tax cuts).

The import content of increased demand varies from countries to country and, *a fortiori,* according to the measure in question. In very general terms it will be higher for income/consumption tax cuts and transfer payments than for other measures (*except* public-sector investment if materials and equipment are procured from abroad). Consequently although tax cuts and transfer payments have a lower overall demand effect than public current expenditure on manpower or goods and services generally, the higher import content of taxes/transfers probably means that the increase in imports will not differ very greatly between these measures. The employment effects in the *rest of OECD* necessarily vary according to the strength of the "adverse" balance of payments effects in the country in question.

To the extent that domestic inflation is reduced (e.g. via indirect tax cuts), competitiveness will improve (assuming a constant exchange rate) and there will be a favourable balance-of-payments effect for the country concerned which will offset the increase in imports induced by the higher level of activity. But such a response is likely to be slow to take effect and relatively small in the short run.

As for *phasing out* tax cuts once employment revives, it is more appropriate to consider an on-off tax change, applicable for a limited period, e.g. an income tax rebate, or a temporary cut in consumption taxes (which might create demand in the short run at the expense of demand later). Public expenditure programmes, unless special contingency planning exists, can be subject to considerable legislative and execution delays if changes in the provision of goods and services or investment are contemplated. They can be difficult to stop or phase out, and involve the risk of waste and weak incentives to plan ahead if the threat of discontinuation exists. On the other hand, expenditure on cash transfers can be responsive if increases are made on an on-off basis (e.g. the U.K. special Christmas bonuses to pensioners in 1974 and 1975).

As for the *value of output* the most that can be said is that tax cuts raise demand for marketable output on the part of the population who presumably want the goods they buy whereas in the case of public spending the case for an increased scale of activity in any particular direction, or even across the board, is a matter of political judgement.

Turning now to *targetability,* general tax cuts such as in income tax or consumption taxes do not directly raise the demand for particular categories of the unemployed. On the other hand, changes in the indirect taxes on goods, the production of which is geographically concentrated (e.g. cars) could have strong regional and sectoral impacts. General expenditure, whether on manpower, goods and services, investment or cash transfers does not normally have strong "targetability" features; on the other hand, increased expenditure on manpower might on occasion be intended to favour particular groups and all expenditure other than cash transfers can be specifically programmed to have a strong regional procurement dimension.

SELECTIVE MEASURES TO RAISE EMPLOYMENT

Given the heavy investment in macro-economic forecasting, the quantification of the employment effects of changes in taxation and public expenditure generally is fairly easily established, although a good deal of purely conventional wisdom is nonetheless involved. However, when we turn to "micro", or selective measures, there are far less generally-agreed data available which evaluate and quantify the effects of selective policies, although there is no shortage of more or less polemical literature advocating this or that scheme. This reflects partly the genuine difficulties in making economic forecasts on the highly disaggregated basis ideally required.

Within the limits set by the available data, this section attempts to indicate the considerations relevant to reaching judgements about the employment effects of certain selective measures. The main possibilities considered here are subsidies intended to raise employment in the private sector and public-sector projects primarily intended to create employment.

Employment subsidies

The main possibilities at the national level are a subsidy in respect of wages generally, a subsidy in respect of labour which otherwise would be made redundant, and a subsidy in respect of additional employment. There might also be a *regionally* differentiated subsidy and/or an *industrially* differentiated subsidy intended to assist particular areas/industries: regional/industry subsidies might be automatic in respect of employment in the designated region/industry or they might be related to labour which otherwise would be made redundant or to additional employment. In each case, there might be differentiation according to sex, age or other characteristics. Additionally, in each case the subsidy might be a flat rate of a proportion of wages. Clearly there are many possible variants and it is not possible here to provide a detailed analysis of every one, but before examining the main possibilities, some general observations are in order.

A general wage subsidy applying to the entire labour force is, in many ways, analogous to a reduction in employers' social security contributions, which has already been discussed and will not be pursued further in this section. However a reduction of employers' social security contributions could also be granted for newly-created jobs. Such a scheme was introduced by France in the second half of 1977 providing complete temporary exemption of employers' social security contributions for creating jobs for youth. This scheme is very similar to an employment subsidy for additional labour and will be further discussed below. A flat rate subsidy (per worker or per man-hour) will discriminate in favour of the employment of the lower paid within a given industry and in favour of industries where wages are relatively low, but represent a high proportion of total costs of production. In these circumstances one might expect a bias in favour of inexperienced, low-skilled labour, or industries where such labour is particularly important. With any wage subsidy there is a danger that it might leak more into higher wage settlements than otherwise would have been the case.

Employment subsidies are sometimes criticised on the grounds that they erode the incentive to improve productive efficiency and postpone the adoption of technologically-superior or less-costly techniques, unlike macro measures such as tax cuts. In assessing this argument it should be borne in mind that insofar as subsidies enable particular industries or regions to modernise themselves more rapidly than otherwise would be the case or insofar as, by helping to preserve employment, they reduce trade-union opposition to technological change, it does not follow that employment subsidies are deleterious on balance. Unfortunately, this is about all that can be said *a priori* as the outcome in practice will vary from case to case; obviously, careful policing of the use to which the subsidy is put can help, to some extent, but if employment preservation/creation is the principal consideration, payment of the subsidy will not exclusively rest on sanctions concerning technological progress or economic efficiency. Eventual withdrawal of the subsidy, if employment prospects generally improve, may also turn out to be difficult and this is an added reason for taking considerable care over the decision on the best means for helping employment[5].

Tax cuts or increases in public expenditure raise employment by creating demand for extra output. Insofar as employment subsidies permit firms to employ more labour than otherwise would have been the case, it is necessary to consider how the demand needed to sustain the increase in potential output arises. One possibility is that output is expected to increase anyway, in which case an employment subsidy might induce firms to retain labour they otherwise would have made redundant in the interim[6] or it might induce firms to bring forward

5. In this respect it is worth noting that the real cost of a flat-rate subsidy fixed in cash terms will be eroded by inflation with the passage of time anyway, unlike a subsidy proportional to wages.
6 If the subsidy is related to workers whom firms declare they were going to dismiss.

the time at which they were going to take on additional labour[7]. In both cases there is an increase in employment in the short run, but the longer-run effects are uncertain, but probably weak. Another possibility is that the subsidy, by reducing wage costs, will improve competitiveness[8], thereby inducing both increased import substitution in the home market and increased export demand. To the extent that this happens, employment in the rest of OECD will suffer (by contrast with the favourable effects induced by tax cuts or increased public spending), although, unless enormous subsidies were involved, this effect should be negligible. Unless either or both of these sources of additional demand[9] arose (i.e. expectation of recovery or competitiveness effects) any net increase in employment in the country concerned would simply take the form of an increase in employment at unchanged output, i.e. reduced productivity. A further, major, possibility is that the *net* increase in employment in the country concerned would be small, subsidised labour being substituted for unsubsidised labour. This could happen either by way of subsidised firms extending their sales (and thereby output and employment) at the expense of reduced sales of unsubsidised firms, or by way of hiring or maintaining of subsidised workers at the expense of unsubsidised workers. In the case of substitution, even if the number of workers in respect of whom the subsidy is paid is large, the genuine net increase in employment might be small. In such conditions the true cost per genuinely additional job could be very much higher than is found by simply dividing the subsidy bill by the number of jobs subsidised.

The above points are taken up below in respect of particular types of employment subsidies.

Subsidies to avert redundancies

A temporary subsidy to firms to induce them to retain labour they would otherwise make redundant can, in principle, raise employment, by comparison with what it otherwise would have been, at very low budgetary cost.

Provided that the subsidy plus the cash value of the worker's contribution to the net output of the firm is at least as great as his wage cost (i.e. wages plus payroll taxes) firms will retain labour in conditions where the value of the worker's output alone is less than the cost of employing him. Inevitably if a subsidy of Y is sufficient to sustain the employment of X workers in this manner who, with no subsidy *at all,* would have become unemployed, a subsidy of less than Y will be sufficient inducement to sustain the employment of at least *some* workers. In other words, a payment of Y simply boosts the profits of firms in respect of those "intra-marginal" workers for whom a smaller subsidy would have been sufficient. But there is probably no way of determining the precise relationship between variations in the size of the subsidy and the number of jobs, especially as most firms will use rule of thumb rather than marginal cost procedures. Further, there is probably no administratively simple way of offering a firm a sliding-scale subsidy per worker which rises continuously as the number of workers (who would otherwise have been made redundant by the firm) rises. Consequently the government has to accept that, in respect of some subsidised workers, a smaller subsidy would have been effective. However, it should also

7. If a subsidy is related to additional employment.
8. At given exchange rates.
9. A third—but more or less theoretical—possibility would be that reduced wage costs might lead to price reductions in the home market and create additional domestic demand in real terms.

be borne in mind that a subsidy to maintain employment also has attraction for firms who otherwise have to face dismissal and re-hiring costs[10].

On the other hand, had the workers been unemployed the expenditure on unemployment-related compensation would have been greater and receipts of taxation and social security contributions would have been lower. Taking these factors into account it is conceivable that the gross expenditure on the subsidy might be wholly or more than offset by return flows.

However, there are a number of caveats which need to be noted. We need to know the source of the additional demand for the output of the subsidised worker which is needed if the subsidy is not to become permanent and simply a potentially very costly alternative to other measures to improve profitability. An expected recovery of domestic or foreign demand has already been noted, but there is also a less desirable possibility: the output of subsidised labour could be substituted for the output of unsubsidised labour elsewhere in the economy, in particular under the assumption of a "given" level of aggregate demand or the even stronger constraint of a restrictive demand-management policy. The greater this substitution effect, the greater will be the cost per job. The greater the subsidy the more likely, and the larger this substitution effect is likely to be, so that increases in the subsidy are likely to be associated with a rising cost per job saved. Again, the longer the subsidy is in operation it seems likely that the probability and size of this substitution effect will increase. A further risk is that of outright abuse: where firms declare workers redundant simply in order to get the subsidy; again, the larger the subsidy and the longer it exists the greater the leakage via abuse.

The U.K. Temporary Employment Subsidy

An example of a subsidy intended to avert redundancies is the United Kingdom Temporary Employment Subsidy. The subsidy was introduced in August 1975 and total expenditure up to March 1978 amounted to £275 million. At present a flat rate subsidy of £20 per week is paid in favour of about 180 000 workers. Payments under the present form of the scheme will continue until March 1979. By then total expenditure over the $3\frac{1}{2}$-year period will amount to £400 million and over 450 000 workers will have been supported at different times. But the number of persons affected by the subsidy does not represent a net addition to employment. Some of the subsidised workers would have been employed anyway and some will displace unsubsidised workers. The lower the ratio of additional net employment to the number of jobs subsidised the larger will be the cost per net job created. It is impossible to determine the size of this ratio with confidence or to identify the extent to which it varies over time. The Department of Employment survey of firms' opinions suggests that 30 per cent of firms have identified a displacement effect in respect of jobs in competing firms. This is not necessarily the same thing as saying that 30 per cent of *jobs* represent displacement; the survey also suggests that the displacement effect increases over time. However, the TES is granted for periods of only 3 months at a time but can be extended up to 18 months for any single firm. It might be prudent to examine the effect of alternative assumptions about displacement effects, which could be in the region of 30 per cent or more than 50 per cent.

10. In some countries, unemployment benefits are paid to workers on short-time employment. Such a scheme is to some extent similar to an employment-maintenance subsidy in that firms can avert redundancies during periods of slack demand. However, a major difference is that a proper employment subsidy paid to the firm is intended to maintain output and employment at the same time, whereas short-time unemployment benefits do not support output.

To the extent that subsidised workers would otherwise be unemployed there will be a saving in public expenditure on unemployment-related benefits; also income tax and social security contributions will be paid in respect of the wages received. The size of these offsets to the gross cost of the subsidy will depend on the earnings of the workers in question, which are below average earnings. (This is to be expected with a flat-rate subsidy, which has a greater impact on lower-paid workers, especially women). Assuming *earnings of £45* per week the offsets might be in the region of £16 in respect of reduced *unemployment*-related benefits, plus £17 *additional income tax* and *social security contributions.* However, the precise offsets will vary with the personal circumstances of the workers in question. These offsets are relevant to genuinely net additional jobs, after allowing for displacement effects. Table 14 shows net costs associated with assumed displacement effects. Bearing in mind the earlier remark that the longer the scheme is in operation the greater will be the likelihood and size of the displacement effect, it might not be unreasonable to assume a displacement effect near the lower end of the above at the beginning of the period of subsidisation rising towards an upper limit by the end of the period, although much will depend on the extent to which TES permanently saves jobs which would otherwise be lost.

Table 14. **UNITED KINGDOM**
Displacement effects and net costs of the
temporary employment subsidy
Gross cost £260 M

Displacement effect (%)	Net cost (£M)	Net cost per job (£)
0	−185	−13 per week
30	−50	−3
40	0	0
50	+35	5
60	+60	6

Source: Secretariat estimates taking into account 270 000 subsidised workers, expenditure of £260 million, and assumed average earnings of £45 per week. These figures are for illustrative purposes only.

TES affects the balance of payments in two main ways:
— Insofar as personal disposable income rises so will expenditure and this will induce increased imports;
— Insofar as the subsidy is actually taken up by United Kingdom export firms and enables them to raise their prices at a lower rate than otherwise would have been possible, TES improves United Kingdom competitiveness (at a given exchange rate).

In the longer term the competitiveness effect would be expected to offset the deterioration in the balance of payments resulting from increased incomes. Further, insofar as TES preserves United Kingdom capacity to export or to avoid imports which would arise if United Kingdom productive capacity were cut back without TES, the subsidy should produce a balance-of-payments gain in the medium term.

Subsidies for additional employment

The previous subsidy was intended to preserve existing jobs; a different approach is to subsidise temporarily the recruitment of additional workers who would not otherwise have been employed. Both subsidies are intended to have the same general effect (more employment than otherwise would have been the case), but there are a number of differences between them. A subsidy for additional employment is particularly dependent on the expectation of a revival of activity; it is expected to bring forward the time at which more workers are taken on. However, if there is the expectation of recovery and if firms are taking on additional labour immediately anyway (which will almost certainly be the case in some firms irrespective of the overall outlook), then the greater is the risk that the subsidy will be paid in respect of workers who would have been taken on in any event. To the extent that this happens, the cost per genuinely additional job will be high and the larger the subsidy the greater the risk. For instance, in conditions of seasonal recovery, the risk of waste through this route are considerable, and it might be less cost-effective than the subsidy to avert redundancies. Also, if there are *deflationary* pressures at work, the "take-up" of a subsidy for additional labour may be small and a subsidy to avert redundancies is probably more appropriate.

Regional discrimination

The most common sort of employment subsidies are those paid in respect of employment in economically-depressed regions. It is not appropriate to discuss here the host of issues more relevant to regional policy per se which are associated with regional subsidies, but a number of general observations are in order. Economically-depressed regions which have above-average unemployment anyway are particularly vulnerable to a national economic recession and a temporary subsidy to avert unemployment has a particularly strong case in respect of such regions. By its very nature, a strictly temporary subsidy cannot cope with the deep-seated problems of depressed regions and a more permanent automatic subsidy is often paid or else a subsidy in respect of additional jobs. The existence of such subsidies to stimulate long-term employment in the regions does not necessarily weaken the case for a subsidy to avert redundancies, especially if a redundancy subsidy is paid to the non-depressed regions.

However, it has already been noted that any subsidy involves the risk that subsidised labour will simply be substituted for unsubsidised labour. In conditions of national recession special regional subsidies of all kinds, especially if they are increased, are particularly vulnerable to this effect, employment in the subsidised regions being substituted for jobs elsewhere. If national economic recovery is foreseen, this possibility will be weaker, but if the alernative to moving to a region with especially attractive subsidies is to cease operations, the substitution effect could be larger; it is not clear, however, whether the regions are improving their relative position in this way or not and, even if this substitution effect is occurring, it might be more than offset by the loss of jobs in industries or firms with an above-average sensitivity to the recession and already located in the regions. Even if substitution does take place, it might be acceptable on the grounds that the loss of jobs in the more prosperous areas is somehow less socially damaging, but in order to make that judgement it is important to know the extent of such substitution and the genuine costs per job involved.

Employment tax credits

A fiscal device with a primary employment objective is the employment tax credit. It is equivalent to a wage subsidy in that it reduces the firm's wage costs. By reducing production costs it induces firms to reduce prices (hence stimulating increased demand and employment), or to expand output or both. Moreover, it may encourage firms to substitute labour for other inputs, although this is unlikely to happen unless the scheme is viewed as permanent.

The Employment Tax Credit recently introduced in the United States provides a tax incentive for creating jobs. Employers hiring additional employees in 1977 and 1978 can qualify for this credit for the tax years beginning in 1977 and 1978. For tax years beginning in 1977 (or 1978), the credit is 50 per cent of the amount by which an employer's wages (as defined in the Federal Unemployment Tax Act, i.e. limited to $4 200 per employee) paid in 1977 (or 1978) exceeds 102 per cent of wages paid in 1976 (or 1977). There are restrictions covering the maximum proportion of total wages creditable and the absolute amount payable in a year, and there are concessions in respect of handicapped employees. Government employment is excluded. A similar scheme has been implemented in Canada. It provides for a deduction from taxes owing of up to $2 an hour over a nine-month period for each newly-hired worker. All the jobs created must be full-time and last at least three months. The employer must certify to the Department of Employment and Immigration that the tax-credit jobs would not have otherwise been created. Workers to be hired are referred to the employer by the public employment service. Priority will be given to workers who are unemployed for at least eight weeks. Similar to an investment tax credit operating at the same time, the employment tax credit is differentiated regionally providing the maximum benefit only in areas of high unemployment.

Investment subsidies

A full discussion of investment subsidies raises issues which lie beyond the scope of this report, but a few aspects of investment incentives warrant brief mention here. Insofar as employment prospects could be improved by more investment, incentives to stimulate investment have a role to play in employment policy. Is is not clear whether in OECD as a whole there can be said to be too little investment relative to available labour, because it should always be possible to adopt more labour-intensive techniques, and to the extent that investment generally is lower than it was, this could be a reflection of the state of demand rather than a characteristic of the returns on investment per se. However, in particular industries in certain countries the available stock of capital and the production techniques associated with it might result in output which is becoming less competitive (whether because of poor quality, obsolescent design or relative cost) in world and domestic markets, so that employment prospects are poor. Under such conditions, investment incentives might improve the ability and propensity of firms to invest and thereby improve the prospects for their workers. But the effectiveness of investment incentives needs to be considered. Insofar as demand prospects are weak, investment incentives might make little impact on firms which are unwilling to commit themselves to further investment at present. Investment incentives in the form of tax relief will do nothing to help firms which have no taxable profits anyway. Outright grants on the other hand are more likely to have an impact, but as they involve no discrimination between profitable and unprofitable firms, the value or the quality of the induced investment might be inferior.

Investment incentives increase the ability of firms to increase their activities by releasing funds for additional capital *and* labour, but at the same time they reduce the price of capital relative to the cost of labour. The first effect raises employment, but the second effect implies capital deepening; on the other hand, an increase in the output of the capital goods industries will improve employment. However, it is not clear what the net effect on employment of increased investment incentives would be. Moreover, the net effect of employment and investment subsidies, which exist side by side in some countries, is obscure: do they simply offset one another in terms of their effects on relative prices, but raise employment

71

via their effect on company profitability? It is certain that, for a given expenditure, the employment effects of one subsidy will involve a lower cost per job than for another subsidy; in the short run the more cost-effective subsidy is likely to be one favouring labour, but in the longer the employment outlook might be better if an investment subsidy is used. Unfortunately, there appears to be no systematic attempt on the part of governments to analyse the relative employment effects of investment and employment subsidies so that for the time being to state the issues is about all that can be done.

Job creation

All government expenditure can be said to create jobs, but that is not its prime purpose. What is involved in a job-creation programme is a set of projects of which the primary aim is to create employment and which cease to operate when the employment situation is generally satisfactory. The work done under this heading might include construction projects which can be started and stopped relatively cheaply and easily as the employment situation changes, or the production of some goods or services might be involved. Administrative overheads should be low and there will be some saving in unemployment benefits and some tax return. However, given the likely nature of the labour involved (low wage, young) the savings in income-related unemployment benefits and the tax return are likely to be fairly small so that the net cost per worker *directly* involved in an industrial subsidy scheme might be lower. On the other hand, private sector subsidy schemes involve the substitution of subsidised for unsubsidised workers and the risks of abuse—which do not arise in a public sector job-creation programme. In particular regions, or for particular groups of employees for whom the prospects are poor, job-creation schemes have a useful role. But in conditions where an upturn is foreseen they are probably inferior to wage subsidies; if no upturn is expected, general reflation is in order and can take the form of massive job creation; but if there are tight constraints on reflationary action, public job creation cannot logically operate on a large scale in any event.

The United Kingdom Job-Creation Programme (JCP)

The JCP is intended to provide temporary useful jobs to those who would otherwise be unemployed. The Manpower Services Commission provides grants to cover the costs of labour-intensive, non-profit projects[11], which are proposed and run by sponsors from the community[12]. The government has asked that priority should be given to young people and that the projects should give priority to environmental improvement and the training needs of young workers. £90 M has been allocated to JCP since it was introduced in October 1975: in its first year 3 900 projects had been approved at a cost of £55 M, creating 41 000 jobs. Most projects last 6-12 months. Given the greater relative importance of young workers in JCP as opposed to TES, the gross cost per job and the unemployment benefit/tax/contribution offsets will be lower than with TES. Assuming a gross cost (wage) of £37 per week, unemployment-benefit savings of £12 and increased income tax plus social-security contributions of £10, the *net cost* per job could be around *£15 per week*. Thus, a gross annual expenditure of £100 M, of which £10 M can be in respect of materials, implies the creation of 47 000 jobs at a *net* cost of £36 M. As for *displacement effects* the nature of the work undertaken

---

11. Wages must account for at least 90 per cent of project costs.
12. For example, local authorities, other public bodies, voluntary associations, private firms.

72

so far (e.g. environmental improvements) and the relatively short duration of the projects, suggests that any displacement is likely to have been negligible so far. But if JCP continues the squeeze on the financial resources of the local authorities who account for the majority of JCP projects, this might lead to some substitution of JCP jobs for regular jobs.

As JCP has no effect on competitiveness, the United Kingdom's capacity to export, or capacity to substitute domestic output for imports, the only balance-of-payments effect will be that induced by the rise in the disposable incomes of the workers involved (plus perhaps some small import content of the materials they use), which might be in the region of £20 M a year.

Public works in the United States

Public works are a normal and regular feature of public expenditure irrespective of unemployment, but in the present context interest focuses on the scope for accelerating public works projects in recessions, for initiating new projects intended to raise employment quickly, and for pre-planning public-works projects suitable for rapid implementation when unemployment rises. However, the larger the proportion of expenditure on the purchase of land, on planning/management facilities, and on construction equipment and materials, the smaller will be the employment impact in the short run. Further, the greater the proportion of expenditure on labour devoted to skilled or scarce labour the smaller will be the employment effect (and the greater the risk of exacerbating inflationary pressures).

The 1971 Public Works Impact Program (PWIP) of the United States was aimed at areas with high unemployment, poverty and out-migration, with special emphasis on small projects that could be quickly put into action. $92 million were spent in this way in 1972 and 1973. In December 1974, Title X was added to the 1965 Public Works and Economic Development Act: eligible projects were to be completed within a year after funds were allocated. In 1975 $500 million was authorised for Title X; the 1976 Public Works Capital Development and Investment Act released $2 billion for public works projects and the programme was extended by $4 billion in 1977.

Costs per job vary considerably between different public works projects depending, in particular, on whether new construction is involved, or simply repair, maintenance and conservation. Annual costs per job can lie in the region of $30-40 000 for new construction and $25 000 for repair. Costs per job for repair, maintenance and conservation in areas of high unemployment can be as low as $11 000[13].

The speed with which public works projects can be put into action is a crucial factor in assessing their role in shortrun employment creation. In 1933 it took over 350 days before 90 per cent of contracts had been awarded, and this was reduced to 100 days by 1938. It took 8 months to commit 90 per cent of PWIP funds in the early 1970s, with half the projects being processed in less than 58 days. The average lag between approval and construction was around 5 months, with projects being completed on average within about 300 days after work had started.

13. See *Temporary Measures to Stimulate Employment,* U.S. Congressional Budget Office. Washington, 1975. Costs are gross, before allowing for flowbacks.

Public Service Employment in the United States

Public Service Employment (PSE) means, in this context, programmes that create temporary jobs in the public sector with the primary objective of reducing unemployment. If the work is genuinely worthwhile, and especially if it involves training, it is better to pay people to work than to remain idle; the lower the wages paid the more jobs will be created.

Jobs under PSE tend to involve work broadly similar to that undertaken by regular government employees and there is a temptation to cut regular programme costs at state and local government levels, by substituting workers financed out of PSE funds from federal resources. Evaluations of earlier programmes have shown considerable rates of displacement which, in addition, are increasing over time. However, 1976 amendments providing for a "project" approach (as distinct from funding regular public jobs) and tightened eligibility requirements have reduced these displacement effects. Preliminary research results show a displacement rate of current programmes of about 20 per cent[14].

The Canadian Local Initiative Programme (LIP)

LIP was announced in 1971 to provide job opportunities for work on socially-valuable projects. The projects had to be non-profit-making, capable of quick implementation, to provide at least 30 man-months of work for those otherwise unemployed; at least 85 per cent of total cost were to be in respect of labour. Over the period 1971-74, $440 million had been spent. Table 15 shows simulations for the period 1971-73: if *instead* of $380 million spent on LIP over this period a similar sum had been devoted either to increased current expenditure on goods and services, or reduced income tax, the effects on employment would have been lower.

Table 15. **CANADA**
Replacement of $380 M expenditure on LIP
by current expenditure on goods and services
or reduced personal tax
Effect on employment (000's)

	1971	1972	1973
Current expenditure on goods and services	−1	−26	−27
Income tax cuts	−1	−32	−34

Source: Jump, Hodgins, Szabo, *op. cit.*

Selective measures: Conclusions

To conclude the discussion of selective measures, the following points emerge. In the short run a temporary employment subsidy could be relatively inexpensive in terms of cost per job after taking into account extra tax revenue and lower unemployment benefits, if firms expect an upturn in activity, if the subsidy per worker plus the value of his output offset the costs of employing him, and if the subsidised workers are not substituted for unsubsidised workers. Unlike work-creation schemes or training, the government is not required to provide

---

14. R.P. Nathan, R.F. Cook, J.M. Galschick, R.W. Long, *Monitoring the Public Service Employment Programme* (Preliminary Report). The Brookings Institution, 1978.

any equipment or materials (which, particularly for work creation, might involve balance-of-payment costs). However, insofar as there is no clear source of additional demand, or there is substitution between subsidised and unsubsidised workers, a temporary wage subsidy loses its appeal—although the precise point at which its cost per job ceases to be lower than for other selective policies needs to be quantified.

Longer-term subsidies are often advocated when the prospects for additional demand are poor, e.g. for particular regions, industries or the country as a whole. But a wholly general, national subsidy makes little sense and regional subsidies in such conditions, insofar as they work at all, involve a high probability of creating employment at the expense of unsubsidised areas. Subsidies to particular industries to improve their competitiveness vis-à-vis foreign products can create additional demand and employment, but at the expense of employment in other countries, although the extent to which they can do this and over what time period is uncertain (depending on such things as leakages into higher wage settlements, the effects of the measures used to finance the subsidy, the supply and demand responses, etc.).

The extent to which investment and employment subsidies complement or conflict with one another or are alternatives does not seem to have received serious attention. An interim conclusion might be that to the extent that they improve profits they are alternatives or complementary (although the strength and timing of the difference in their employment effects is obscure); while their different effects on the relative prices of labour and capital are ostensibly conflicting, any increase in the attractiveness of capital deepening as a result of an investment subsidy creates employment in the capital goods industries; in particular countries with uncompetitive or obsolescent productive technologies there is a strong case for additional investment to secure employment over the longer term. Beyond these somewhat obvious remarks it is difficult to go at present.

Public employment-creation projects (except additional public-service employment) are probably more costly than a temporary wage subsidy with a low substitution effect, but the more deep-seated and long-term the employment problem the greater the relative attraction of job-creation schemes. However, national job creation is an alternative to general reflation and assuming a relatively low priority attached to the goods and services produced by work-creation projects general reflation will be superior; but if there are constraints on general reflation, work-creation projects cannot make a significant impact on employment. They are probably most suited to creating employment in particular regions or for particular groups of workers where private demand is low and where subsidies would either be ineffective or would involve significant substitution effects.

THE MEASURES COMPARED AND THEIR APPROPRIATE MIX

As far as the *employment effects* are concerned, for a given financial cost additional public service employment is generally the most cost-effective measure in the short-term (see the simulation results for the United States in Table 14). However, a temporary employment subsidy to avert private sector redundancies can be even quicker acting and might involve a lower cost per job, but this clearly depends upon whether or not firms find the subsidy worthwhile, whether demand is expected to recover shortly, and the extent to which subsidised labour is substituted for unsubsidised labour. The longer the subsidy is in operation the weaker its effects. An increase in public expenditure on goods and services will be somewhat more costly per job than an increase in expenditure on manpower alone; expenditure on construction projects will have uncertain but probably weak employment effects unless a great deal of prior preparation exists, in which case they might be regarded as examples of job-creation schemes which often involve low costs per job (although not as low as increased manning in existing public service programmes and perhaps not as low as a temporary redundancy subsidy). Next highest in terms of cost-per-job is probably increased expenditure on cash transfers to low-income households, followed by cuts in income and indirect taxes. Reductions in corporate profits tax or payroll taxes are likely to be uncertain in their short-term employment impact and probably weak.

The *timing* of the effects on employment is important. A temporary subsidy against redundancies can be quick acting but its effects wear off in time. Public expenditure on manpower, goods and services or transfer payments are somewhat slower to have an impact but the effects grow over time; direct and indirect tax cuts take even longer to have an impact but again the effects grow over time, so that relative costs-per-job vary with the time horizon.

The *quantification* of the effects of tax and non-selective expenditure measures, while difficult, can nonetheless usually be achieved more easily on the basis of available macro-economic models than in the case of selective measures. However, if governments are concerned with demonstrative effects, it is a fairly simple matter to collect information on the direct employment effects of selective measures, such as subsidies or public employment creation, whereas estimates of their indirect impacts on the negative side are difficult, if not impossible, to make.

A major difference between tax or general expenditure measures and subsidies is that the former work by first *raising demand* in the economy, whereas employment subsidies are most effective in protecting or increasing employment if demand is expected to recover. A further major difference is that tax or general expenditure measures in a given country raise demand for the output of other countries; insofar as subsidies raise demand in a given country by improving the competitiveness of particular industries, this might well be at the expense of other countries.

As far as *inflation* is concerned, a cut in indirect taxes, assuming it is passed on, will have the largest direct effect. To the extent that wage subsidies are intended to sustain employment by subsidising wage costs no impact on prices is likely to result[15], but insofar as the intention is to improve the competitiveness of "traded" goods, some reduction in the rate of inflation is possible (unless the package of measures is intended simply to alter relative prices between traded and non-traded goods by imposing extra taxes on the latter to finance the subsidies, although the distinction between the sectors is blurred); however, wage subsidies, whether it is intended that they should be reflected in prices or not, involve some risk of inducing higher wage demands and reducing management resistance to wage claims. Reductions in income tax or increased cash transfers might moderate wage claims but this is far from certain. Quite apart from these influences, there is the possibility of a "Phillips Curve" effect resulting from sustained or higher employment which will vary with the employment effects of the measures. In this respect, a temporary wage subsidy against redundancies is attractive, if demand is expected to recover, as it works by immediately reducing redundancies but has a weakening employment effect later.

In terms of *balance of payments* effects, wage subsidies to the private sector probably have the smallest adverse effect in the country in question and, insofar as they are used to improve competitiveness, might have a beneficial

---

15. It being assumed in this case that in the absence of the subsidy there would be reduced employment instead of higher prices.

effect (account being taken of the various caveats noted above). Public job-creation projects could have a relatively strong adverse effect, depending on the extent to which complementary materials and equipment need to be imported. As for tax and general expenditure measures, the difference is uncertain because, while the import content of extra private demand induced by tax cuts is larger than in the case of increased public spending, the total demand effect of the latter is greater.

Turning to *allocational* considerations, selective policies can have significant effects in the longer-run. Subsidies may weaken incentives to modernise and adopt more efficient techniques—unless they help to allay worker resistance—although they raise the ability of firms to finance change. Selective measures are often intended to improve the prospects of particular regions or industries, although in the former case this might be at the expense of employment in unsubsidised areas. As for reallocation of employment between industries, much will depend on the means adopted to finance the subsidy, the extent of leakages into higher wage settlements and the relative supply and demand responses.

The above analysis shows that no single global or selective measure could be used as an "ideal" instrument responding to every possible set of circum-stances. And even if the circumstances were very similar, countries would be likely to make different choices between policy instruments, reflecting differing priorities as to the relative advantages and disadvantages of the various instru-ments. But the policies outlined above are best regarded not as alternatives, but as complementary parts of an overall employment policy package, each measure having a different role to play. Different sets of circumstances and different priorities would, thus, translate into a differing emphasis in the mix of programmes.

However, a number of generalisations seem possible and useful, given the fact that virtually all OECD countries currently face the unsatisfactory hesitancy of general economic recovery and a bleak outlook for employment over the medium term. A first important conclusion to be drawn from the above analysis is that selective measures on the whole are more effective in raising employment in the short term than general macro measures *having the same cost*. However, the employment effects of tax reductions tend to grow over time, whereas the employment effects of certain selective measures, notably subsidies against redundancies, will gradually wear off. Relative costs per job will, thus, vary with the time horizon. Nevertheless, given the expenditure ceilings to which most governments are committed over the coming years, the greater short-term cost-effectiveness of selective measures clearly represents a major advantage.

In the case of countries with weak balance-of-payments positions, an addi-tional advantage is the lower import effect of selective measures to stimulate employment, as compared with macro measures. A further major advantage of selective job-creation measures is their targetability. By their very nature, they can be directed towards improving the employment prospects of particular groups, regions or industries more readily than general macro measures. This targetability makes selective demand measures, in principle, less inflationary than global ones (this, in particular, holds true under certain conditions for wage subsidies), but anti-inflationary effects may also result from income tax reduction (via reduced wage pressures) and an even more direct price-reducing effect will result from cuts in indirect taxes. On the whole, therefore, the analysis has not led to conclusive results on whether or not selective job creation is clearly less inflationary under present conditions than global stimulative measures.

Against the three major advantages (comparatively low budgetary and balance-of-payments costs, and targetability) stand the potential major disadvan-tages of selective job-creation measures in that they may weaken incentives to modernise industrial structures and technologies (through employment subsidies to the private sector), or result in extra output for which there is no clear demand (direct job creation in the public sector). Micro-measures, also, tend to have a weaker impact on employment in the OECD area as a whole than macro-measures, because their spill-over into imports tends to be smaller. These negative effects are likely to increase the longer the measures are in use. From this it must be concluded that micro-measures are mainly useful on a temporary basis, for instance as part of a recovery strategy. They are less relevant and may, under certain conditions, even become harmful if they are continued during a long period of time, but not accompanied by global demand stimulation. This conclusion is particularly relevant for employment subsidies applied to the private sector which will only be effective in anticipation of an expected revival of aggregate demand. Whether or not additional output resulting from job-creation measures in the public sector will be acceptable and sustainable over a longer period is, to a great extent, a matter of political judgement and will vary to a large extent between types of public sector programmes.

Within the framework of a short-term recovery strategy, there should be a different mix of selective and global measures as between groups of countries. Countries with high import elasticities and prompt wage and price reactions should consider giving more weight to selective job stimulation in their reflationary policies than strong countries in which a relatively greater emphasis on global measures would have beneficial effects for trade expansion in the area as a whole. The importance of temporary selective measures will and should diminish over time once a more general expansion gets under way.

While selective job stimulation by private-sector subsidies or public-sector programmes are primarily relevant for short-term recovery strategies, they need not necessarily be useless or harmful in a medium-term strategy. The above observation on the structural risks associated with long-term subsidies or public employment programmes rather points to a situation in which measures which have been designed as short-term employment protection measures are being carried through into successive years as if they were *de facto* medium-term policies. In the next chapter it will be shown that selective stimulation of the demand for labour can also play a significant role in a sound medium-term employment and manpower strategy (though a less important one than for a short-term recovery strategy) *provided* the measures are responsive to the under-lying structural trends and shifts of the employment system as discussed in Chapter I of this report.

Chapter IV

MEDIUM-TERM POLICIES TO COUNTERACT STRUCTURAL IMBALANCES IN THE EMPLOYMENT SYSTEM

A short-term recovery strategy—while essential for achieving self-sustained growth performance—is unlikely to be sufficient to regain full-employment. The analysis in Chapter I has shown that the labour market of the 1970's is considerably different in structure from that of the 1960's. In particular, the length of the current recession is going to lead to growing intractability of the unemployment problem. Therefore, even selective demand expansion itself, whilst being a necessary condition, is not a sufficient condition for removing all the structural imbalances that have occurred to the extent that is necessary for bringing unemployment down to acceptable levels. In particular, demand expansion may be incapable of reversing employment problems, such as access to employment for less-competitive groups, and long-duration unemployment; and it may be incapable of significantly reducing unemployment resulting from increased movements of people in and out of the labour force, inflationary pressures resulting from the shift of employment to the tertiary sector, and unemployment resulting from dissatisfaction with certain kinds of jobs. A medium-term employment and manpower strategy will, therefore, require a very broad mix of policy responses. These will include measures affecting the demand side of the labour market as discussed in the previous chapter (i.e. employment subsidies and public-sector job creation), as well as traditional manpower-adjustment measures. Furthermore, the nature of certain labour-market problems will require additional policy responses which lie outside the usual framework of employment and manpower policy instruments.

Effective medium-term policies include those which recognise the need for continuing measures to offset factors which adversely affect the balance of labour supply and demand in the medium-term. The purpose of this chapter is to bring these longer-run structural considerations to bear on policies now being adopted or considered. Such an analysis, however, encounters the major difficulty that the situations of Member countries differ widely concerning the characteristics of these structural changes. These differences are greater than for short-term cyclical analysis, as Chapter I has demonstrated. Nevertheless, an attempt is made there to identify a few *common* structural shifts and problems in a number of OECD countries. The present chapter will take these findings as a starting point. Of necessity, the discussion will need to remain fairly general, directed at the kind of problems which appear to emerge in the OECD area as a whole, it being understood that structural policy measures for individual countries will require more intensive analysis and adaptation at the national level.

Chapter I gave evidence of a trend rise in the rate of unemployment since the late sixties in a majority of OECD countries and of the emergence of a certain number of structural labour-market imbalances. These imbalances, in part, explain the trend rise in the rate of unemployment. But there are other structural problems emerging which do not necessarily result in higher rates of unemployment, yet need to be considered when designing medium-term policies. The various structural issues identified in Chapter I will be regrouped and appropriate policy responses dealt with under four major headings: measures tailored to particular groups in the labour market; policies to counteract frictional and mismatch unemployment; measures to reduce relative labour costs, and policy responses outside the usual scope of employment and manpower policies.

MEASURES TAILORED TO PARTICULAR GROUPS IN THE LABOUR MARKET

Two categories of the labour force have been identified as the most severely affected by previous adverse employment experiences and medium-term prospects: youth, having increasing difficulty in entering employment after leaving the educational system, and the long-term unemployed who become more cut off from the world of work the longer they stay out of it. In the latter category also fall (mostly older) workers who have withdrawn from active job seeking and, thus, no longer show up in recorded unemployment figures. The number of persons affected by long-duration unemployment, therefore, is probably higher than is shown in the statistics. In the case of youth it is important to note that failure to gain access to the labour market for several years can mean lost training opportunities that may not be regained at a later date, or if they are with increased cost and difficulty. As in the case of older workers, the process of being unemployed for a considerable period of time may be largely irreversible or reversible at a much greater cost to society than that of policy measures that can be currently initiated. These two groups should be accorded the highest priority, in view of the serious decline in individual welfare, social costs which continue to rise and the danger of the irreversibility of the process of unemployment. Women are also encountering difficulties in finding suitable jobs if no special efforts are undertaken. Finally, migrant workers involuntarily leaving their host countries normally remain unemployed, and face severe setbacks to their standards of living, whilst at the same time adding to the economic problems of their home countries.

It should be observed that the groups referred to in the previous paragraph are not the "disadvantaged" in the traditional sense, i.e. the physically or mentally handicapped, school drop-outs, ex-prisoners, etc. The special employment problems of these traditional groups stem partly from the way the labour market normally operates, and frictions and structural imbalances will further work against them. However, policy instruments to deal with the handicapped in the traditional sense, such as rehabilitation measures and sheltered workshops, are not considered in the present report[1].

Direct and indirect job creation will continue to be a significant element of any policy package dealing with the two high-priority groups—unemployed

1. For a detailed discussion, see Harish C. Jain, *Disadvantaged Workers in the Labour Market in Selected Member Countries*, OECD, forthcoming.

youth and the long-duration unemployed[2]. The risk of generating additional wage and subsequent price pressures by inserting these groups into employment would appear to be low, given their limited bargaining power and degree of union organisation. It would make both social and economic sense to reserve job-creation in the private sector mainly to youth via employment or training subsidies. This would permit gainful employment and work experience which is essential for enhancing career prospects. On the other hand, job creation in the public sector, with the government possibly acting as "an employer of last resort" could be developed with emphasis on the long-term unemployed and, in particular, elderly workers who tend to be crowded out of the market. A clear separation along these lines, however, is not imperative. Youth unemployment in particular needs to be attacked also by public employment-creation schemes. But a guiding principle in developing public youth pro-grammes should be to "invest" in youth, i.e. to provide young people with experience and knowledge which is supportive in their further development. It would be socially counterproductive to insert youth into public "make-work" arrangements which would lead to dead-end jobs and the dulling of initiative, or which would diminish their chances of finding jobs elsewhere because of employers' hiring practices.

Public-sector job creation has been subdivided in the previous chapters into 3 main groupings: public works, public sector employment and special public employment programmes. Public works have been described as being not selective enough, lasting too long and difficult to initiate, too difficult to phase out when the general economic climate improves, and too capital- and skill-intensive; they are, in short, expected to feed inflation...". The extension of public sector employment has been, and will be, severely constrained mainly by a concern with the strong growth of bureaucratic structures in the past. However, the latter argument would not hold in the case of providing youth with such opportunities as summer jobs in traditional public services or for creating youth organisation such as conservation or peace corps. The third group of measures, special public employment programmes, can also be designed in different ways and the traditional image of "make-work" arrangements no longer appears to be correct for describing recent developments in this area. In several countries, such programmes have, in recent years, been modified considerably by decentralising the initiative for programme administration to local communities or voluntary group level. Considerable job opportunities could be created both for unemployed youth and the long-term unemployed, provided there is sufficient public acceptance and active support and co-operation at the local level.

If job-creation schemes for the target groups of youth and the long-term unemployed are to be successful they need to be supplemented and supported by manpower adjustment, in particular training schemes. Training measures have been the subject of critical reviews and, as was dealt with in an earlier chapter, this was further accentuated by the fact that the present lack of employment opportunities cannot be solved by short-term solutions on the supply side of the market. However, medium-term measures to counteract rising trends of labour market segmentation against youth and the long-term unemployed can hardly be conceived without a major reliance on investment in human capital with the intention of raising the competitive advantage of these

2. Comprehensive policy packages to deal with youth unemployment have been reviewed in great detail elsewhere. See: *Youth Unemployment.* 2 volumes, OECD, forthcoming.

special groups. The foreseen continuation of high rates of unemployment suggests a major effort in training the unemployed, but in view of the underlying labour-market trends it is equally relevant to regard training, further training or re-training of the employed as a significant element of a medium-term strategy.

Training is useful not only for increasing, but also for restoring human capital. Over time, human capital depreciates—the longer one remains away from school or work the greater the depreciation. Refresher courses or recurrent education programmes for the employed as well as the acquisition of skills in growth occupations for the unemployed, can be useful in offsetting this tendency towards depreciation. Ideally, individuals themselves would make these corrective investments, but severe financial constraints in the case of the unemployed and family responsibilities or pressing work demands in the case of the employed may always be prohibitive. Consequently, public involvement is required if for no other reason than to offset these constraints which inhibit the ability of individuals to invest in themselves. But since returns accrue largely to individuals, consideration could be given to cost-sharing mechanisms—at the very least, tuition charges might be considered the responsibility of the individual. To ensure that the poor have adequate access to training, consideration could be given to subsidy schemes which could also be designed to permit individuals to shop around for what they perceived to be the best training bargains.

For youth, the transition from school to work needs considerable support through public programmes within the formal education system to ensure adequate preparation for the requirements of the world of work. Those leaving the school system should preferably have a variety of options which provide for a transition to working life. A combination of classroom training, on-the-job training and work experience still requires greater development in most countries. Training facilities for the long-term unemployed need to be tailored to the particular needs and characteristics of the unemployed and adjusted to the kinds of jobs to be created by both the public and private sectors for these groups. For both target groups, specialised vocational guidance, counselling and placement efforts would appear to be of particular importance. These measures need to have an "out-reach" component, both for the persons in need and the employers (private and public) who are expected to hire youth and longer term unemployed. The "out-reach" to employers would be of particular importance in cases where the failure of disadvantaged groups to find jobs is not primarily related to their individual shortcomings but has its roots in discriminatory hiring practices by employers. For the individual, "out-reach" is especially important to those who have lost their confidence or who have withdrawn from the labour force or who simply do not know how to obtain relevant labour market or manpower adaptation information.

For a more vigorous endeavour to insert or re-insert these two target groups into private sector employment, there is also the possibility of adjusting wage differentials, which for a variety of reasons may have got out of line with their relative productivities. This could be achieved in different ways: reducing payroll taxes; providing wage subsidies; by income policies; or by a combination of these measures. Some observations on reducing relative labour cost to foster employment will be given below. The main aspect to be noted in the context of youth and long-duration unemployment is the possibility of using these measures to tilt hiring decisions in favour of these target groups. It is, however, important to emphasize that these measures may well improve the employment situation of these groups at the expense of other

82

groups unless employment as a whole is expanding. The main result achieved would thus be a more equitable distribution of employment opportunities. An unresolved issue is to what extent corrective measures in relation to wage differentials can be sustained over a long period without generating pressures to restore differentials through the collective bargaining process.

Particular work-sharing measures tailored to the special problems of youth and long-duration unemployed have also been considered in a number of countries. But as indicated in the introductory chapter, measures to regulate or to reduce the supply of labour, of which work-sharing schemes form part, go beyond the scope of the present report.

For the two other target groups mentioned above, i.e. women and migrant workers, the problems are quite different from the groups discussed so far. The strong non-cyclical rise in female participation rates is one of the most dynamic factors which has and probably will continue to affect the labour market in a fundamental way. Strong overall economic growth would be the only completely effective means to increase work opportunities for women as strongly as in the past. Given the constraints on growth, it is highly likely that major concern will arise in relation to rising female participation rates and the issue will need to be put into a much broader social and political context. An extremely difficult policy task will be to formulate policies relating to labour supply which will not discriminate by sex in achieving equality of access to limited employment opportunities[3].

Migrant workers and their home countries are the most severely affected by the world recession. Emigration countries have to face the negative effects of declining world demand for their domestic production in addition to the return of emigrants and the reduced outflow of workers resulting from the economic slowdown in host countries. The change in economic relationships resulting from the turnaround in migration policies suggests the need for an adjustment process in the emigration countries which can be facilitated by intensified international co-operation. For example, returning migrants could be assisted to integrate into their home economy through appropriate inter-national agreements[4].

POLICIES TO COUNTERACT FRICTIONAL
AND MISMATCH UNEMPLOYMENT

The likelihood of a continuing rise in frictional and some kind of mismatch unemployment is prompted by three analytical findings documented in Chapter I:

— Over the past decade or so a job-creation process has been occurring in the tertiary sector, particularly favouring job seekers coming from outside the labour force (notably women), whereas job opportunities in other sectors of the economy that traditionally recruit from inside the labour force, remain stable or are falling. In spite of a steady overall growth in aggregate employment (except in 1975) therefore, recorded unemployment tends to persist even in periods of rapid growth. This occurs because during upswings the service sector

3. See also: *The 1974-75 Recession and the Employment of Women*, OECD, 1976.
4. These and wider issues of economic co-operation between immigration and emigration countries are being considered in other work of the Organisation. See: *Migration, Growth and Development*, Report by a Group of Independent Experts, OECD, forthcoming.

tends to recruit a greater percentage of its workers from outside the labour force than does the goods sector, which recruits proportionately more from the ranks of the unemployed.

— The increased share of women and teenagers in the total labour supply, plus the more unstable nature of their employment leads to higher turnover or frictional unemployment. Also, since women and teenagers are apparently remaining in the labour force in periods of economic slack in greater numbers than formerly, partly because of unemployment compensation and partly because of greater commitment, there are higher rates of recorded unemployment today during each downswing.

— There is also evidence for some countries that there are today larger gross labour flows in the market, in many cases as a result of the factors listed above. These increased flows can, in themselves, produce increased levels of "frictional" or "turn-around" unemployment—some of which is of a chiefly short-term voluntary nature, but some of which is more serious.

The single most serious problem appears to be the disequilibrium between jobs created in the tertiary sector, which to a large extent are filled by new labour force entrants on the one hand, and a declining number of jobs in the industry sector increasing the number of unemployed on the other. Whilst this issue has wider implications for policy (related to the long-term rise in the total labour supply), there also appears to be an important mismatch aspect between sectoral supply and the demand for labour. It is not likely that displaced workers from the industry sector are always suited to fill the job openings available in the tertiary sector, nor are the often lower wages particularly attractive, at least at the outset. The question, therefore, must be raised as to what extent any adjustment can be achieved. Apart from a wide range of placement, counselling and guidance services provided through the public employment exchange, the main remedy appears to be retraining programmes for the unemployed and preventive measures to encourage "general" as distinct from "company-specific" vocational training. But if the lower wages in the tertiary sector are the main cause, then training measures would not be of great value either. In fact, no particular adjustment measures, except the adjustment of wage differentials themselves, would appear to be suitable at all.

In contrast to fixed physical capital, labour can always quit the firm, in which event not only is the training investment lost to the firm, but the returns may actually accrue to a competitor. Consequently, firms have a natural tendency to limit training to those skills which are specific to the job the trainee will fill. Further, since there is uncertainty as to whether employees will remain on the job long enough for the training to generate a return, there is an incentive to underinvest even in very specific training. In practice, the market applies a correction to this tendency by shifting backward at least some training costs to employees in the form of reduced wages. But this correction is likely to be imperfect.

In spite of these natural market tendencies and in spite of rising need for sectoral and occupational mobility, however, there are a number of reasons why it is desirable to encourage training in enterprises, rather than in institutions. Empirical evidence suggests that on-the-job training, with its practical orientation in a working environment, generates larger returns (as measured by future earnings streams) than institutional training. These factors suggest that governments might consider subsidising firms to provide more general training than they would if guided by market trends. However, since it is difficult to ensure that such subsidies are used for the desired training objectives, firms may treat them as unconditional grants and in no way alter their training patterns. Consequently, this strategy may lead to difficult administrative problems.

An alternative way to induce firms to increase their ratio of general to specific human capital investments would be for unions to adopt an objective of this sort in their collective bargaining strategies. In fact, a number of West European countries (notably the United Kingdom, France and Italy) have formed tripartite boards with representatives of unions, management and governments to oversee company training efforts. One limitation to this approach is that unions themselves may be wary of more generalised training efforts due to jurisdictional restrictions (viz., members of one union receiving training in another's skill). Where this is no restriction, consideration can be given to a tradeoff between reductions in working hours and training. For example, instead of bargaining for an unconditional reduction in working hours, unions might consider asking for the hour equivalent to be passed along in the form of training, perhaps through job rotation as well as through some classroom instruction. This would be responsive to the objectives of spreading work and providing training of a diversified nature and yet would meet management objectives of ensuring that training be somehow firm specific.

However, formal off-the-job training in public institutions for adults, in particular retraining for the unemployed, will also continue to play a major role over the medium term in assisting workers to move from industry to tertiary sector jobs. But it has to be acknowledged that to the extent that displaced industrial workers compete with peripheral workers, not too much can be expected to be achieved from the above training efforts. The competitive advantage of the peripheral workers is their greater mobility, their desire for part-time or short term contracts and their acceptance of lower wage rates. One—albeit relatively minor—step in the right direction would be legislation to make part-time work subject to the same unemployment conditions as full-time work.

A major issue for medium-term policy consideration is the question of whether and to what extent increased frictional unemployment is of a voluntary nature. In the above analysis a non-cyclical trend of rising frictional unemployment was partially explained by the rising labour market share of women and teenagers characterised by less job attachment as well as by increased gross flows, mainly between inactivity and gainful employment, thus leading to more spells of unemployment. While accepting that some of this unemployment is probably of a voluntary nature, the above analysis also observed that there was no statistical evidence for a rising trend of quits (as distinct from dismissals) in countries where this information is available. This circumstantial evidence therefore gives no support to the thesis that voluntary job changes and intermittent job-search unemployment can explain much of today's higher level of frictional unemployment.

Even if more voluntary turn-around unemployment occurs there are no grounds for public authorities to diminish their efforts to assist people in the job-search process through the public employment service. In the past decade this service has been extended in many countries so that its operations and services cover the entire work force. This has often been a difficult task given the low image of this service in the past. However, during the recent recession the functioning of the service has again been criticised, partly because of its limited role as a labour exchange in a situation of mass unemployment, and partly because the increased work load resulting from unemployment-benefit payments has limited its deployment of other services such as labour market monitoring and counselling. In terms of medium-term strategy for employment and manpower policies, it would be a serious setback if the public employment service were to be reduced to its earlier role of an "unemployment office" serving only a marginal group of disadvantaged job seekers and firms looking for unskilled workers. This being said, it is also true that under present conditions of large-scale unemployment the service should address itself preferentially to groups with special labour-market problems.

According to some observers individuals' expectations in relation to qualitative job characteristics are lacking, whereas the actual supply of jobs does not show a corresponding improvement in job quality. No statistical evidence is available which would explain some of the present unemployment by a mismatch of job aspirations. However, a mismatch may not manifest itself directly in higher recorded unemployment but in job dissatisfaction and may be expressed in other forms (absenteeism, work stoppages, reduced productivity) which also represent waste in economic and social terms. For the medium term it is relevant, therefore, to take timely action even if it may be of secondary importance to raise job quality in times when the predominant concern is with a severe overall shortage of jobs. Job restructuring, new types of work organisation and enterprise manpower planning will certainly need to be further developed. If governments fulfill a major role in raising the productivity of the work force through training, retraining, and recurrent education, there would seem to be a corresponding need to initiate and favour developments in the private enterprise sector, i.e. by appropriate action on the demand side, which would permit a better matching of work aspirations and job openings. One possibility for government intervention referred to earlier is the employment exchange which should monitor and assist employers to adopt advanced manpower planning and job restructuring in response to the characteristics and aspirations of job seekers. In areas where the government acts as an employer, there is wide room for experimenting with and improving work organisation and career development programmes. Finally, governments could support efforts to improve the quality of working life through the collective bargaining process, at least indirectly[5].

REDUCING RELATIVE LABOUR COSTS [6]

Chapter I referred to some evidence suggesting that a rise in the cost of labour relative to capital user costs in industrialised OECD Member countries may have occurred in recent years. Such evidence is extremely sensitive to exactly what is included under "costs" and the time periods covered in the analysis. More importantly, however, it is not entirely clear whether rising relative labour costs (if that is really what is occurring) are due to longer-term structural phenomena as opposed to conjunctural declines in aggregate demand. It is well known that productivity (output per person-hour) and thus unit labour costs are strongly responsive to movements in output. As output begins to rise from a cyclical trough, employment is

5. For more details see K. Walker and R. Shore, *Towards Policies for Life at Work*, OECD, 1977.
6. The following discussion leaves aside any policy intervention in the collective bargaining process and other forms of wage determination. These issues are dealt with in *Socially Responsible Wage Policies and Inflation*, OECD, Paris, 1975.

increasing with a lag so that productivity jumps and unit labour costs fall. Conversely, when output falls, productivity falls correspondingly and unit labour costs consequently rise. These patterns result from normal lags in labour adjustment and they occur independently of movements in relative wage rates. It is therefore not clear how much of the apparent rise in relative labour costs is due simply to depressed aggregate demand which would be reversed with economic expansion.

But independent from demand effects, it is likely that a drop in relative labour costs should increase labour's employment prospects over the medium term. More specifically, there are three kinds of costs which policies can be designed to affect in order to stimulate employment: hiring, carrying and firing costs. Regarding *all* these components, governments can change existing policies which adversely affect costs or they can introduce new policies to realign costs in a more favourable (to employment) fashion. Examples of the former would be reductions in taxes on payrolls (social security, unemployment insurance taxes); examples of the latter would be special tax incentives (e.g. depreciation allowances for labour).

Hiring costs can be lowered by reducing the costs to firms of searching for particular kinds of labour. Employment services help to perform this function. Computerised job listing, bonding and certain licensing practices are other examples. The justification for public intervention in this area (aside from the presumed social nature of the benefits of increasing employment) is that there are economies of scale to be realised in the collection and provision of information about employment possibilities; i.e. individual firms cannot gather the requisite information as efficiently as a single agency, such as the government.

Carrying costs are those which accrue whether labour is productively employed or not. Some of these costs are fixed. Safety devices to reduce industrial accidents and certain fringe benefits are illustrations of fixed labour costs. Some of the costs are "quasi-fixed"[7] in nature; that is, they are stated as a proportion of wages which themselves may be only partially adjusted for actual hours of productive work[8]. Examples of these would be social security and unemployment insurance taxes and, of course, wages themselves. Clearly, the higher these carrying costs are (and some evidence of their growing share in total labour costs has been quoted in Chapter I), the smaller will be the stock of labour which producers are willing to maintain. In particular, when there is considerable uncertainty about likely future demand such as occurs in conjunction with the kind of unstable growth of recent years, relatively high carrying costs imply lower employment of labour.

It is sometimes argued that payroll taxes, such as social security and unemployment insurance, are shifted back on to labour in the form of reduced wages (or forward in terms of higher prices). There is disagreement about the proportion of these taxes which is actually shifted backward, some authors arguing that it is 100%, some 50% and others 0%. Empirical evidence is by no means conclusive. To the extent that backward shifting is complete (100%),

7. W.Y. Oi, "Labour as a Quasi-Fixed Factor of Production", *Journal of Political Economy*, December 1962, pp. 538-555.
8. While wage costs may or may not accrue for days absent from work, depending on individual circumstances, they *are* usually paid as long as the employee shows up for work *whether or not* a full day is actually spent in productive work. Obviously, there are exceptions to this generalisation (e.g. piecework, construction), but they are probably becoming fewer in relative terms.

it would imply that decreases in such taxes would have zero effect on employment—changes in taxes would be met with corresponding counterchanges in wages, and total labour costs to the employer would be unaffected. Whether this is likely to occur cannot be decided on theoretical grounds. With marginal productivity more or less constant, producers can either pass along tax cost increases in the form of lower wages or by reducing (or not increasing) employment. The same wage bill and total product can be attained no matter which strategy is selected. However, workers are likely to press employers to choose the latter alternative to the extent that they do not perceive an immediate threat of redundancy since in this case the costs are shifted outside the immediate workplace onto the unemployed.

This view of the process suggests that increases in payroll taxes (or any other elements of the carrying costs of labour) will be harmful to employment in the aggregate. In particular, if capital is not subject to the same kinds of levies, payroll taxes will raise the costs of labour relative to other factors and perforce imply a reduction in labour's share of employment. It is further implied that any reductions in the *ratio* of fixed to total labour costs, apart from their levels, would be employment-stimulating. Apart from these general observations it is difficult to make appropriate proposals for policy. In Chapter III the short-term stimulation of employment via reductions in payroll taxes was regarded as not very effective compared with other measures. However, over the medium term there would appear to be more grounds for assuming positive employment effects due to changed price relationships between capital and labour and a reduction in the ratio of fixed to total labour costs. Of course, how stimulative such policies might be is an empirical question which cannot be answered on the basis of available evidence. There are data suggesting a certain downward inflexibility of wages which implies that employment, rather than wage rates, is likely to be the principal adjustment mechanism for achieving equilibrium in the labour market[9].

The final cost element to be considered is the cost of dismissing labour; that is, the ease with which a given labour redundancy can be corrected. Some countries have legislated dismissal costs, others have allowed collective bargaining agreements or custom to determine their levels. In the United States, the unemployment insurance system is "experience-rated", so that firms with a relatively large number of successful claimants per insured tax base have to pay a higher tax rate to the unemployment insurance fund—this, in an effort to discourage layoffs. In Western Europe, severance pay is a prevalent phenomenon, in some countries averaging something like 16% of annual earnings. In Japan, the customary lifetime contract sets a very high dismissal cost, effectively pre-empting the firm's right to lay-off redundant labour[10].

Very high dismissal costs, while they protect continued employment rights for individuals, also reduce the employment prospects for the unemployed. Obviously, an employer who realises that he may have to absorb the costs of carrying redundant labour will be reluctant to hire that labour initially unless prompted by an optimistic view of the expected demand for output. In other words, high lay-off costs imply high hiring costs, *ceteris paribus*. A tradeoff appears to exist between the objective of stabilising employment (through increasing costs of dismissal) and increasing its level.

9. Robert Haveman, "Unemployment in Western Europe and the United States: A Problem of Demand, Structure or Measurement?" in *American Economic Review,* May 1978.
10. Further evidence is provided in Chapter I.

POLICIES OUTSIDE THE USUAL SCOPE
OF EMPLOYMENT AND MANPOWER POLICIES

Not all structural issues identified earlier can be adequately dealt with by traditional labour-market policies, i.e. by manpower adjustment and job-creation measures. The shift of employment from industry to the tertiary sector has been described as one likely source of inflationary pressure due to rigid wage relationships, associated with diverging productivity trends between the two sectors. It is important to note that manpower-adjustment measures are limited to making this shift as smooth as possible, but do not remove the inflationary pressures. To the extent that governments have resorted to restrictive demand-management to contain these inflationary pressures the outcome is lower employment for the economy at large. It follows that the appropriate policy response in this particular case may neither be found in general demand-management, nor in selective employment and manpower policies, but rather in the area of incomes policy. However, considerations of prices and incomes policies are beyond the scope of the present report.

Chapter I has identified a continued increase of female and peripheral labour force participation coupled with strong job-creation in the tertiary sector, but stable or falling job opportunities in the other sectors that have traditionally provided jobs for the existing labour force. This process has been closely related to the expansion of the public sector, where the kinds of jobs created may correspond more closely to the kinds of jobs increasingly sought: part-time jobs for married women; research and teaching jobs for university graduates; sheltered jobs for the disadvantaged, etc. The pronounced intention of several governments to impose ceilings on the future growth of public expenditure will seriously reduce the employment prospects for the above groups of workers, and one of the major sources of past job creation will generally dry up. There may, of course, be a reversal of past trends in that productivity gains in the manufacturing industry might become slower (possibly induced by slower wage-cost increases) and that the manufacturing sector in the future might again absorb more labour than in recent years. It has also been argued that a slower growth of the public sector would create room to stimulate, via demand management, a correspondingly stronger growth of the private sector. However, in terms of employment creation, the results could be very different: the number of jobs created per additional output would be much smaller in the private sector (assuming higher relative productivity levels) and the kinds of jobs offered would not necessarily correspond to the aspirations of the bulk of new labour market entrants.

Given the possibility of a growing labour supply, coupled with a slow-down in demand, some rather fundamental questions concerning the future role and meaning of work and employment need to be raised. What should the full-employment concept correspond to in modern industrial societies? Does the employment/unemployment dichotomy any longer respond to the realities of choice and preference as between full-time work, part-time work, formal education, training, leisure, retirement and other options? While many agree that significant changes in this area are taking place, there is neither a meaningful concept nor a quantitative indication of changing attitudes and values vis-à-vis work and non-work which could be used as a guide for policy. Yet for any future growth policy, a clear conception and quantification of the goal of full employment, the social values associated with work and with the various alternatives to labour-market work, would be essential.

Given these uncertainties, governments will probably adopt a trial-and-error approach in steering policies between socially-desirable and economically-appropriate solutions. These, on the whole, will fall into two categories. The first category will include measures which in one way or the other reduce or regulate the supply of labour. One approach already adopted by several European governments consists in erecting various impediments to immigration and the hiring of foreign workers. There is also the whole range of policies to reduce working time, such as increased school attendance and lower retirement age. The other group of measures, on which the present report has mainly been focused, comprises all those which aim at bridging the gap between labour demand and supply by increasing demand. General growth, trade and investment policies belong to this category. But assuming that such policies will not achieve the full-employment goal, it has been suggested by some that it may be necessary to change the contents of growth by deliberately discriminating in favour of the expansion of labour-intensive industries. This would imply a policy boosting the demand for labour over and above the level induced spontaneously by economic development. It could be achieved by appropriate industrial and regional development strategies or by subsidisation of small enterprises and labour-intensive modes of production.

It is, however, unclear whether this strategy would create the kind of jobs increasingly looked for. This leads back to the question of the appropriate role to be played by the public sector. Proposing to create jobs in the public sector without due regard to the public services to be produced and the impact of financing them is, of course, of limited value. However, criticism could also be raised against proposals that suggest stopping the growth of the public sector merely on the ground that it is becoming too big and withdraws too many resources from the private sector. A conclusive answer as to what would be the optimal size can only be found by considering the demand for public services and the problems of financing them, such as growing tax resistance and post-tax wage pressures[11]. Furthermore, consideration should be given to the possibility of strengthening the employment impact of a given level of public expenditure. In this context it would also be conceivable to streamline and reorganise bureaucratic and cumbersome administrative structures that would permit a re-allocation of labour in the public sector with the intention of providing new public services:

— in areas where social needs are still urgent or are likely to become so (certain sectors of health, environment protection, urban planning and transportation, programmes for the elderly);

— in areas which are more or less directly improving the efficiency of the private sector (labour market information and placement, maintenance work and renovations of public infrastructure such as telephone and other communication systems, highways, airports, etc., industrial training);

— in ways which leave more room for private initiative and which are drawn up and administered on a decentralised basis.

---

11. C.A. van den Beld, for instance, has demonstrated on the basis of an econometric model for the Dutch economy that further growth of the public sector would increase the cost-burden of the private enterprise sector so that labour-capital substitution in the private sector would outstrip job creation in the public sector. See: "Employment growth in the Collective Sector versus the Enterprise Sector", in: *Structural Determinants of Employment and Unemployment,* Vol. II, OECD, forthcoming.

SUMMARY AND CONCLUSIONS

The medium-term employment outlook is particularly difficult and un-certain because:

— inflationary and other constraints may require governments to main-tain relatively cautious demand management policies over the medium term allowing only a slow reduction of unemployment;

— earlier hopes for a recovery of economic activity which would put OECD economies back on the track towards a satisfactory medium-term growth path have not so far been realised;

— due to much built-in labour slack the time lag between renewed expansion of output and the reduction of recorded unemployment is likely to be longer even after a sustained recovery commences;

— the "full employment-unemployment rate" in many OECD countries has tended to rise over the past few years primarily because of increases in the total supply of labour, as well as its changing composition especially towards women and teenagers;

— the longer the depressed business climate continues, the more unem-ployment is tending for many people to become irreversible.

One main cause of current unemployment is the demand deficiency for goods and services produced. Consequently, little can be done to solve the problem in a fundamental and lasting way before a recovery of aggregate demand gets underway. However, there are a number of reasons which suggest that the revival of demand would be a necessary but not a sufficient condition for making rapid progress in reducing unemployment. A number of structural imbalances now exist in the labour market which will make the process of employment recovery slower than would have been the case say, 10 years ago. A reduction in unemployment will, therefore, require greater policy efforts in the future than would have been required in the past.

Bearing in mind the immense social and economic costs of high and prolonged unemployment and having regard to the 1976 Recommendation of the OECD Council on a General Employment and Manpower Policy which reaffirmed the achievement of full employment as a policy goal, there is an urgent need to reconsider the proper role of unemployment and man-power policies within a general and non-inflationary full-employment policy. The identification of medium-term labour market trends and the formulation of a medium-term employment and manpower strategy which is responsive to these trends should serve this end.

There has been an underlying trend of rising unemployment since the late 1960's in a number of OECD countries. This upward trend can be explained partially by the build-up of structural imbalances in the labour market.   Under conditions of persisting demand slack these imbalances are likely to worsen, implying a growing intractability of the unemployment problem over the medium term.   Some significant factors explaining the rising trend in unemployment are the following:

— A continuing increase in female labour-force participation coupled with strong job-creation in the tertiary sector, that particularly favours women, has accompanied stagnating or declining job opportunities in the other employment sectors of the economy traditionally providing opportunities for other groups.   Consequently, in spite of a steady overall growth in aggregate employment (excluding 1975), recorded unemployment has tended to persist even in periods of rapid employment growth.   This results because during an upswing the service sector tends to recruit a greater percentage of its workers from outside the recorded labour force than does the goods sector, which recruits more from the ranks of the unemployed.

— The increased share of women and teenagers in the total labour supply, and lower job attachment by these groups, leads to higher turnover and frictional unemployment.   Also, since women and teenagers are apparently remaining in the labour force in periods of economic slack in greater numbers than before—partly because of unemployment compensation and partly because of a greater commitment to labour-market activity—there are higher rates of recorded unemployment today in each downswing.

— Labour-exporting countries face a special labour market problem because of returning migrant workers and a sharply reduced outflow resulting from the economic slowdown and a change in the migration policies of the labour-importing countries.   This makes it increasingly difficult for aggregate labour demand to match supply.

— Whether or not there has been a non-cyclical trend of rising labour costs relative to capital costs, possibly leading to an accelerated substitution of capital for labour, is difficult to establish empirically. In several countries there may have been some longer-term decline in profitability as real wages increased relative to the value of output. Moreover, labour costs other than wage costs appear to have risen substantially in many countries and labour has increasingly been turned into a quasi-fixed factor notably as a result of increased dismissal costs.   These factors have in all likelihood induced firms to operate with a smaller labour stock for a given level of output and have slowed down capacity and employment-extending investments.

— There is also evidence for some countries that larger gross labour flows now exist in the market, in many cases as a result of the factors listed above.   These increased flows can, in themselves, produce increased levels of "frictional" or "turn-around" unemployment—some of which is of a short-term voluntary nature, but some of which is more lasting and involuntary.

The report also identifies certain other employment problems which, while they in most cases only indirectly relate to the non-cyclical rise in aggregate unemployment, nonetheless require special policy responses in the context of a medium-term employment and manpower strategy:

— The increasing duration of unemployment (even when adjusted for the higher aggregate rates) is leading in many cases to the labour force discouragement of older workers as witnessed by falling participation rates, and suggests a growing irreversibility of the unemployment/employment process at the upper end of the age range. This problem will become more important in coming years as the demographic picture changes to include more elderly people.

— There is growing labour-market segmentation along age lines, working to the particular disadvantage of youth (both sexes, and especially first-time job seekers). Failure to gain access to fairly stable employment opportunities in the labour market for several years can mean lost training opportunities for youth which may not be regained at a later date, or if so only with increased cost and difficulty. As in the case of older workers, a lengthy period of unemployment, or intermittent employment for youth, may be largely irreversible, or only reversible at a much greater public cost than would apply if corrective action is currently taken.

— The continuing influx into the labour force of "peripheral workers", i.e. those who may have a relatively lower job and labour-force attachment such as secondary family workers, students, retired persons, raises the issue of what is the proper total number of paid job opportunities to be provided as a goal of full-employment policy.

— There is reason to believe that problems of job dissatisfaction and qualitative job mismatch may possibly be disguised but not removed during the current recession. While job dissatisfaction may not result directly in an increase of recorded unemployment, there are other ways (absenteeism, work stoppages, reduced productivity) through which dissatisfaction can be expressed.

— The aggregate rate of unemployment may increasingly mask large dispersions within specific rates by age group, sex, race, occupation and region. Moreover, the aggregate rate is becoming of limited use as an indicator of labour demand pressures (because of other forms of labour-market slack), and as an indicator of wage-push pressures (because of the relative lack of trade-union organisation and seniority among the groups whose unemployment has increased the most, i.e. youth, women and part-time workers). Policies based solely on the aggregate rate, therefore, may not achieve their desired affect.

In reviewing manpower policies since their implentation in the early 1960's it is important to realise that their main initial purpose was to facilitate economic growth. At least in Europe, economies were under continuing tight labour market pressures and the concept of an active manpower policy was adopted on the ground that it would facilitate manpower adjustment to economic and technical change, and that it would increase the productivity of the labour force and tap additional manpower resources. The situation was somewhat different in North America where economies operated at considerably higher rates of unemployment. Here, a major objective of manpower policies was to raise the employability and the job opportunities of the more disadvantaged and thus, to contribute to social equity. In both cases policy-makers were guided by long-term considerations. Major extensions and innovations occurred in adult training and retraining programmes, and fundamental reforms were introduced to improve the functioning of public employment services.

In the late 1960's and early 1970's policy-making was increasingly overshadowed by creeping inflation and a continuous deterioration of the trade-off between inflation and unemployment. A number of policy advisors (including the OECD) urged governments to adopt selective manpower policies as a short-term device to counteract cyclical swings in employment. As these measures were held to be anti-inflationary, they could be of considerable advantage as compared with global anti-cyclical measures which were becoming increasingly difficult to regulate accurately because of the unstable unemployment-inflation trade-off. However, with the noteworthy exception of Sweden, this anti-cyclical concept did not gain much ground in policy-making or proved institutionally difficult to implement. The idea of using large-scale training courses during periods of economic slack and thus to reduce unemployment was supported by some but was criticised by others as a way of disguising unemployment.

The 1974/75 recession created a new challenge to these policies because the economic slump was much more severe and prolonged than in any period after World War II. The main policy line adopted by the majority of countries facing declining demand and output was to encourage the maintenance of existing employment to the extent possible, and to maintain the income of those who became unemployed. Not adopted as a major strategy was an effort to counteract declining employment by creating new employment in either the public or private sectors. The basis attitude, thus, was a defensive one characterised by the intention to cushion the economic hardships of the recession for those directly affected. The consequences of these policies pushed unemployment forward and placed its burden onto those entering the labour force, especially youth and women, and created substantial labour slack which weakened the linkage between increases in output and hirings.

At the present time, with the belief in a self-sustained upswing receding more and more into an uncertain future, traditional manpower policies have to face increasing difficulties. Job-creation measures often cannot reduce total unemployment on a permanent basis merely by achieving a net increase of jobs. Substitution and replacement effects may nullify the effectiveness of these measures and simply lead to a redistribution of unemployment (which of course may be desirable in some cases). It has also been observed that job-creation often pulls a great number of newcomers into the labour market instead of absorbing the existing unemployed to the extent anticipated. To the extent that the earlier decline of output was cushioned by employment protection measures in the private sector, there is now a risk of creating some undesirable side-effects, such as impediments to structural change and technological innovations, if these measures are extended over too long a period of time. Manpower-adjustment measures, while of considerable importance during the upswing, are also of reduced effectiveness during a prolonged period of economic slump given the weak demand conditions in virtually all labour markets.

While these constraints on manpower policies are presently affecting the majority of Member countries there are some cases, e.g. the United States and some European countries, where considerable progress has been made in improving or stabilising the unemployment situation. In these countries, selective employment and manpower policies have been closely co-ordinated with general demand-management policies. It should be recalled that such coordination was one of the main principles of the 1976 Recommendation of the OECD Council on a General Employment and Manpower Policy: "The objectives of employment and manpower policy, the emphasis on policy instruments, and the manner in which these instruments are employed, all are affected by variations in the level of economic activity. In view of this, it is essential for governments to improve the interrelationship of overall economic policy with employment and manpower policy to ensure that their fundamental complementarity enhances full achievement of the objectives of both"[1].

Selective policies—in particular direct job-creation measures—should therefore be set within a more general framework of macro policies and other policies designed to stimulate non-inflationary growth and raise employment. For this reason, the report has undertaken a comparative assessment of global and selective job-stimulation measures, dealing basically with taxation and non-selective expenditure measures on the one hand, and employment subsidies to private industry and direct job creation in the public sector on the other.

The most important conclusion to be drawn from this analysis is that, given their quick and direct impact on employment, selective measures are mainly useful on a temporary basis. Countries which opt for reflating their economies could consider including in their reflationary package a strong element of selective job stimulation, notably by means of employment subsidies to the private enterprise sector. This would probably speed up the reduction in unemployment over and above what could be expected from a general revival of aggregate demand. Notably weak countries characterised by high import elasticities and prompt wage and price responses would be strong candidates for large-scale job stimulation of this nature. In strong countries, an emphasis on global measures would have more beneficial effects for trade expansion in the OECD area as a whole. The need for temporary selective measures will, and should, diminish over time once a more general expansion gets under way.

Countries experiencing continued sluggishness of aggregate demand will be faced with the problem that employment subsidies to the private sector involve structural risks within countries and for trade between countries, if they are pushed too far and rolled forward in consecutive years over a longer period of time. These risks would seem to occur if essentially short-term employment protection devices are rolled forward during the current persisting recession—as if they were *de facto* medium-term policies. Subsidies to prevent redundancies or subsidised short-time working, for instance, may provide greater incentives to weaker firms than to stronger ones which, over the longer-run, may led to undesirable factor allocations and industrial structures. A more appropriate emphasis of selective measures under conditions of general demand slack is probably job creation programmes in the public sector—tailored to groups and areas which are most affected by the recession and containing a strong element of investment in human capital.

In the medium-term there is a need for continuing measures to offset adverse structural shifts affecting the balance of labour supply and demand. They comprise a set of co-ordinated measures operating both on the demand and supply sides of the market. Additional policies outside the traditional employment and manpower policies are also required (such as income policies, policies affecting participation in the labour force and the distribution and allocation of working time, educational policies, etc.).

In the analytical part of this report, two groups have been identified as having particularly severe labour-market problems of a structural kind— youth and the long-term unemployed. Policies to deal with these groups could include employment and training subsidies favouring youth, and public-sector employment measures directed to the long-term unemployed. For youth the most essential requirement is to achieve a foothold in gainful employment.

---

1. *Ministers of Labour and the Problems of Employment,* Vol. I, page 77. OECD, 1976.

In instances where special government employment programmes are developed for youth, it is important to ensure that the type of work and the work experience provided support the further development of the careers of youth, and that enrollment in these programmes does not lead to subsequent discrimination in hiring by private employers. Other policy instruments include those facilitating the transition from education to work, "out-reach" measures for placing the long-term unemployed in employment, and various training measures which would raise the competitive advantage of these groups.

Increasing frictional and mismatch unemployment appears to be resulting from three sources: employment generation is tending to become restricted to the tertiary sector which, predominantly, recruits from outside the labour force; the labour force share of women and teenagers with relatively lower job attachment is rising; gross flows of labour into the market or between an active and non-active status are rising. Some of the types of unemployment resulting from these trends are voluntary, but others are involuntary and require appropriate policy responses.

A most difficult problem of balancing the growth of employment in ways which effectively reduce unemployment results from the fact that jobs created in the tertiary sector are filled by *new* labour force entrants, whereas jobs displaced in the industry sector lead to rising unemployment. Displaced industrial workers are usually not suited to filling the openings provided by the tertiary sector and policies to facilitate rehiring of industrial workers in the tertiary sector appear to be somewhat limited in their potential effectiveness. The main instruments available are longer-term retraining courses for the unemployed, and measures to encourage general as distinct from highly-specialised vocational training as a preventive device. More generally, there is a problem of labour market adjustment arising from the growing importance of the "peripheral" labour force.

Placement services and related measures for facilitating job search and more rational hiring procedures will be required continuously over the medium term. Increasing market friction needs to be counterbalanced through an efficient and comprehensive public employment service. Enterprise manpower planning and "internal labour market policy" require co-ordination with public employment policies, in particular in local labour markets. Job dissatisfaction, while not necessarily manifesting itself in higher unemployment, may lead to other forms of human and economic waste. Over the medium term, therefore, there appears to be a rising need for supporting efforts to match job content to a greater extent with worker skills and aspirations.

A reduction in labour costs would increase employment prospects in the future, although a marked effect on levels of employment is unlikely if the recovery of demand is slow. A downward adjustment could occur through the collective bargaining process, but for various institutional reasons is likely to be too slow in its effect. Policies designed to stimulate employment by modifying hiring, carrying or dismissal costs of labour, therefore, merit objective review. Hiring costs can be lowered by reducing—through the public employment service—the costs to firms of searching for and selecting labour. Among the various elements of carrying costs (i.e. those which increase the fixed or quasi-fixed nature of labour costs), payroll taxes appear to be the most amenable to policy measures. High dismissal costs, while they protect continued employment rights for individuals, also reduce the employment prospects for the unemployed. Obviously, an employer who realises that he may have to absorb high dismissal costs will be more reluctant to hire additional labour in the first place. There appears to exist a trade-off, therefore, between the objectives of employment security and employment expansion.

Given the possibility that economic growth over the medium term may not be sufficient to increase employment as rapidly as the labour force is likely to grow, and that real wage developments will not lead to sufficient market clearance, there are two broad categories of policy responses possible:

1. To reduce or regulate the supply of labour, for instance, by relating educational, training and retirement opportunities to work opportunities in such a way as to facilitate more flexible patterns of working life, education, leisure and retirement.

2. To increase labour intensity at any given level of economic activity by appropriate industrial and regional development strategies.

The latter category would also include a strengthening of the employment impact of a given amount of public expenditure, as well as a further extension of the (generally more labour-intensive) public sector relative to the private sector.   However, this strategy may not be viable in countries in which the public-sector share has reached a level at which it impinges on the growth performance of the economy.   In these instances, it might be preferable to adopt policies to initiate—with a relatively small financial involvement on the part of the government—employment-creating activities in the private or community sectors which respond to new types of demand in fields such as environmental protection, energy saving and social services.

Annex I

SUPPORTING DIAGRAMS

Diagram 1

LABOUR FORCE, EMPLOYMENT AND UNEMPLOYMENT IN THE OECD AREA

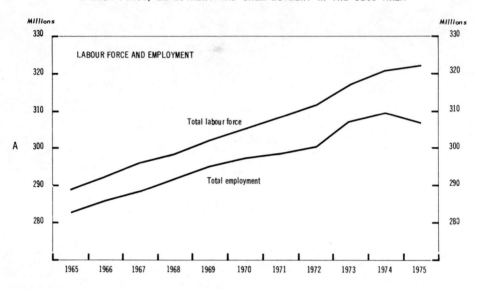

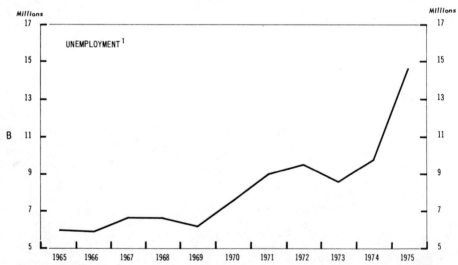

1. Excluding Portugal, Greece and Turkey, countries for which unemployment data is not available over the period.

Sources : OECD Labour Force Statistics.

Diagram 2
UNEMPLOYMENT RATES ADJUSTED TO U.S. CONCEPTS
IN SELECTED INDUSTRIAL COUNTRIES 1960-1976

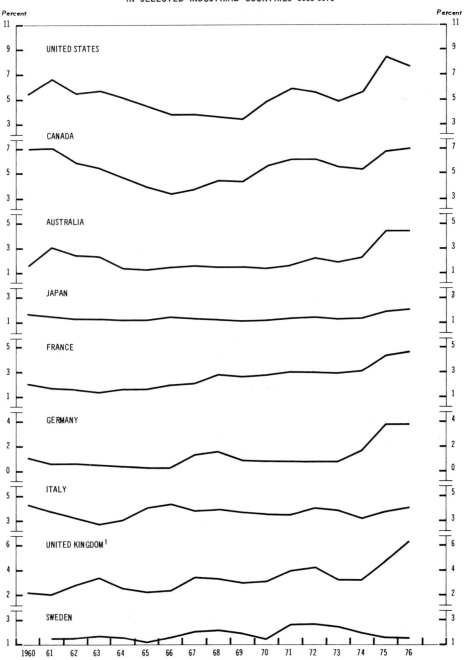

1. Great Britain only.
Source: U.S. Bureau of Labour Statistics.

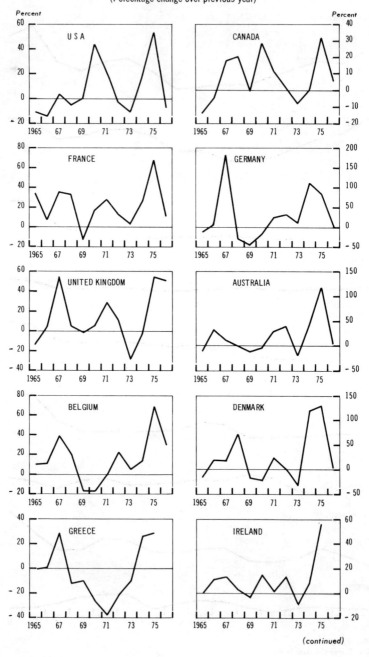

Diagram 3

RATE OF GROWTH OF UNEMPLOYMENT
IN SELECTED OECD COUNTRIES 1965-1976
(Percentage change over previous year)

(continued)

102

Diagram 3 (continued)

RATE OF GROWTH OF UNEMPLOYMENT
IN SELECTED OECD COUNTRIES 1965-1976
(Percentage change over previous year)

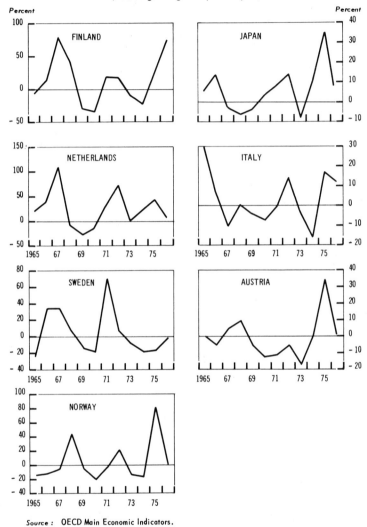

Source : OECD Main Economic Indicators.

Diagram 4
VACANCY AND UNEMPLOYMENT RATES
(as a percentage of total labour force)

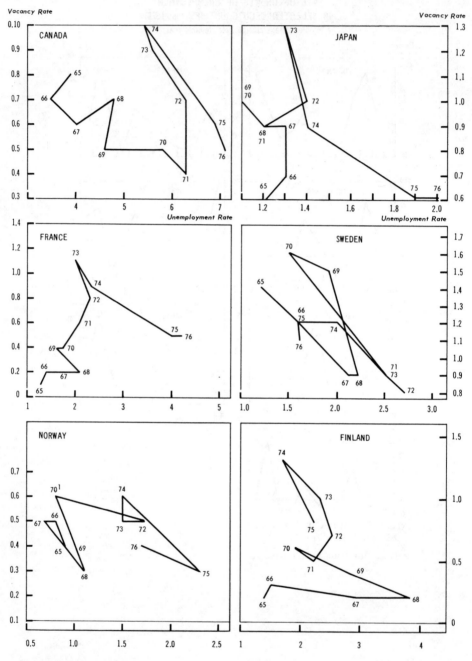

1. Data for 1971 not available.

Sources : OECD Labour Force Statistics, OECD Main Economic Indicators.

Diagram 4 (continued)

VACANCY AND UNEMPLOYMENT RATES
(as a percentage of total labour force)

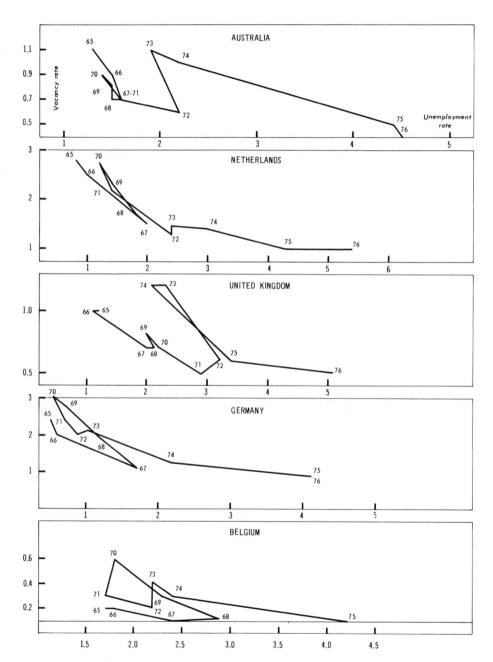

Sources : OECD Labour Force Statistics and OECD Main Economic Indicators.

105

Diagram 5

POTENTIAL LABOUR FORCE (——) AND POTENTIAL EMPLOYMENT (---→)

(three year moving average, 1955-1973)

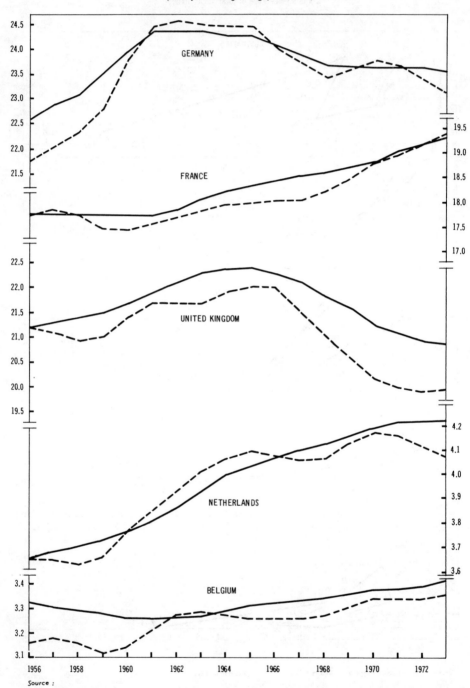

Source :

Wim Driehuis, "Capital-Labour Substitution and Other Potential Determinants of Structural Employment and Unemployment", in: *Structural Determinants of Employment and Unemployment,* Vol. II, OECD, forthcoming.

Diagram 6

AVERAGE ANNUAL GROWTH OF CIVILIAN LABOUR FORCE AND EMPLOYMENT
1965-1975
(averages of percentage change over previous year)

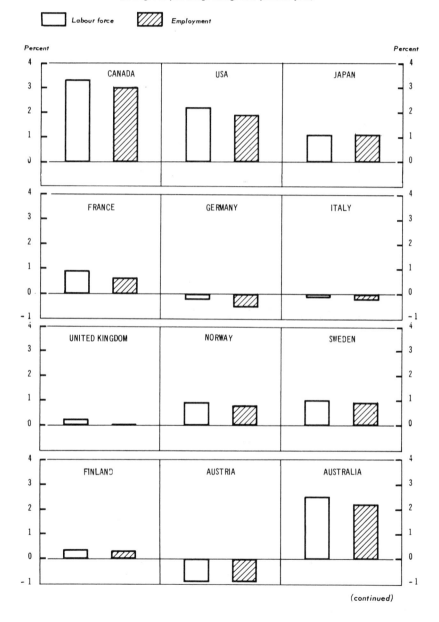

(continued)

Diagram 6 (continued)

AVERAGE ANNUAL GROWTH OF CIVILIAN LABOUR FORCE AND EMPLOYMENT
1965-1975
(averages of percentage change over previous year)

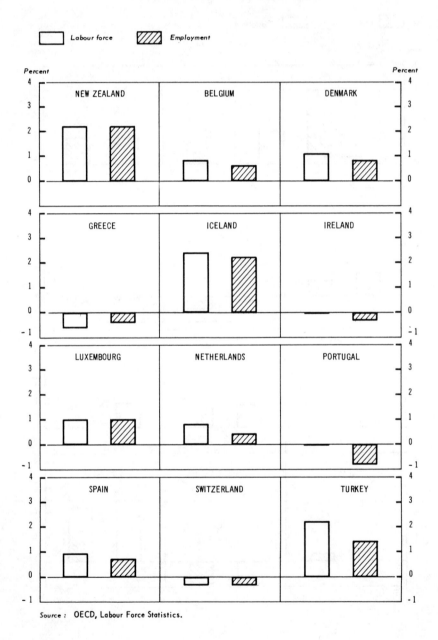

Source : OECD, Labour Force Statistics.

Diagram 7

CONTRIBUTION OF EACH SECTOR TO CIVILIAN EMPLOYMENT GROWTH IN OECD COUNTRIES 1965-1975
(weighted percentage change over previous year)

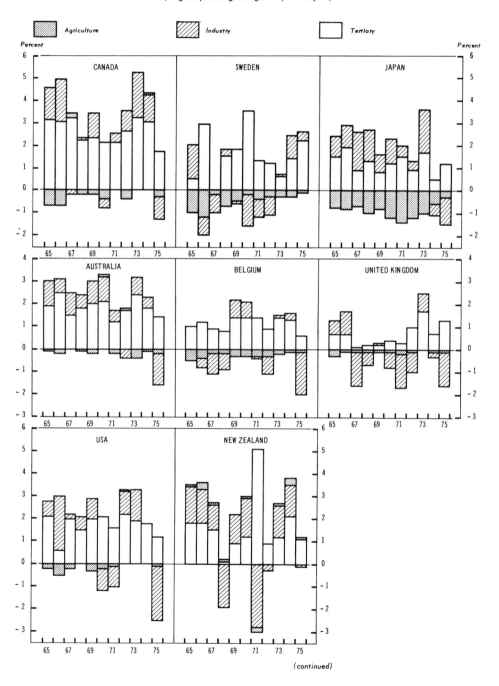

(continued)

Diagram 7 (continued)

CONTRIBUTION OF EACH SECTOR TO CIVILIAN EMPLOYMENT GROWTH IN OECD COUNTRIES 1965-1975
(weighted percentage change over previous year)

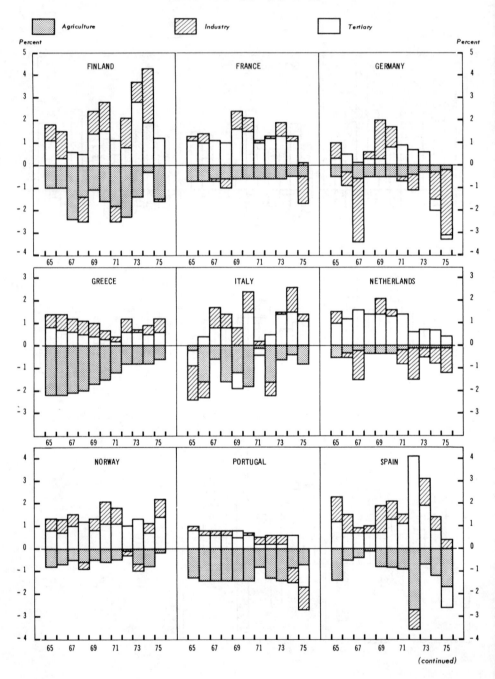

(continued)

Diagram 7 (continued)

CONTRIBUTION OF EACH SECTOR TO CIVILIAN EMPLOYMENT GROWTH IN OECD COUNTRIES 1965-1975
(weighted percentage change over previous year)

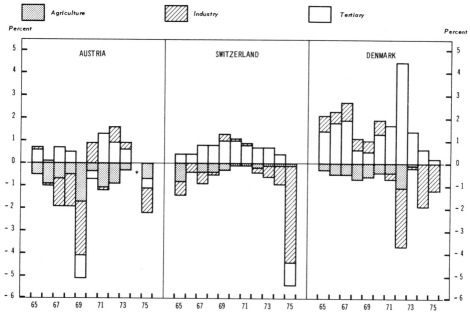

* Not available.

Source : OECD Labour Force Statistics.

111

Diagram 8

RATIO OF POPULATION AGED 15-64 TO TOTAL POPULATION

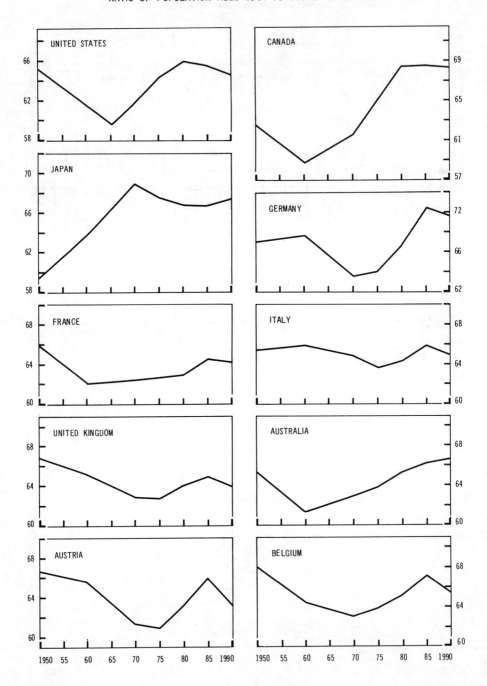

Diagram 8 (Contd.)

RATIO OF POPULATION AGED 15-64 TO TOTAL POPULATION

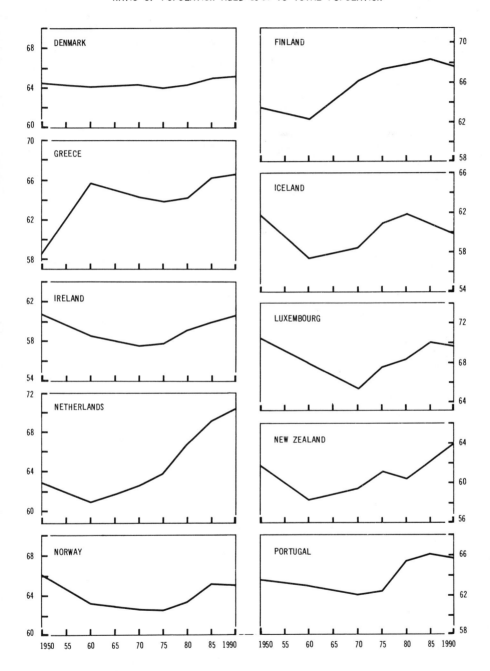

Diagram 8 (Contd.)

RATIO OF POPULATION AGED 15-64 TO TOTAL POPULATION

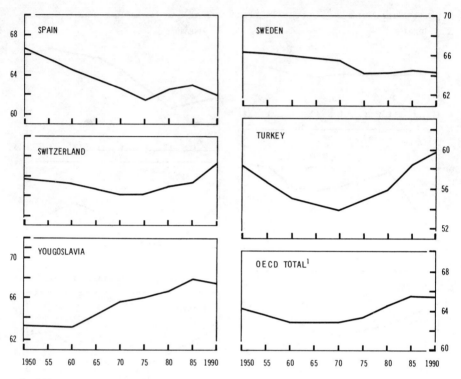

1. Arithmetic average.

Sources : OECD Labour Force Statistics and Secretariat projections.

114

Diagram 9

MIGRATORY MOVEMENTS IN WESTERN EUROPE

Net migration to labour importing countries   Net migration from labour exporting countries [1]

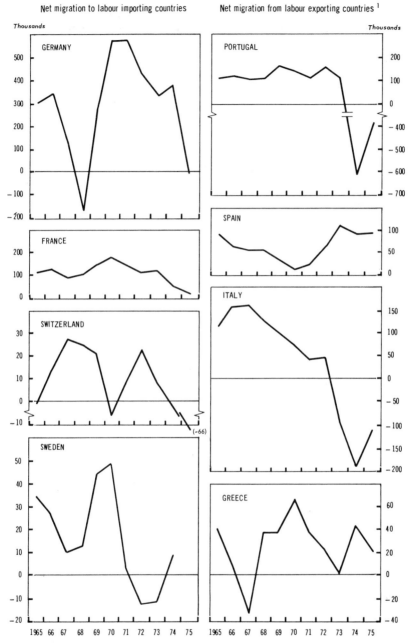

1. Turkey is equally an important labour exporting country. However comparable data is not available. The OECD Economic Survey for Turkey (August 1976) gives following data in thousands for Turkish emigration :

1967	1972	1973	1974	1975	1977 (Plan estimate)
5	67	136	20	4	50

Source : OECD Labour Force Statistics.

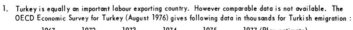

115

Diagram 10

RATE OF LONG DURATION (over 6 months) UNEMPLOYMENT
AND AGGREGATE UNEMPLOYMENT RATE (as a percentage of total labour force)

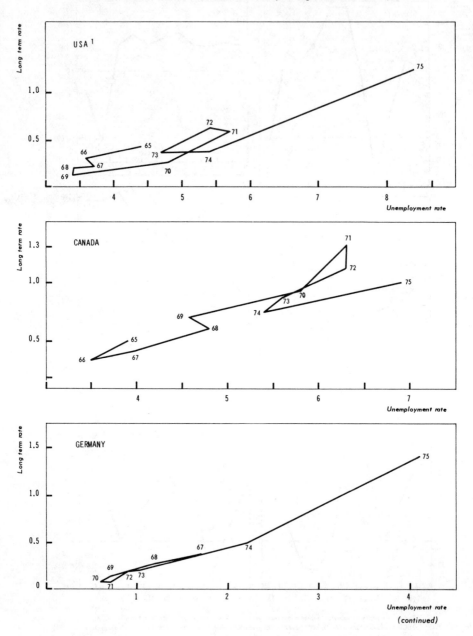

(continued)

Diagram 10 (continued)

RATE OF LONG DURATION (over 6 months) UNEMPLOYMENT
AND AGGREGATE UNEMPLOYMENT RATE (as a percentage of total labour force)

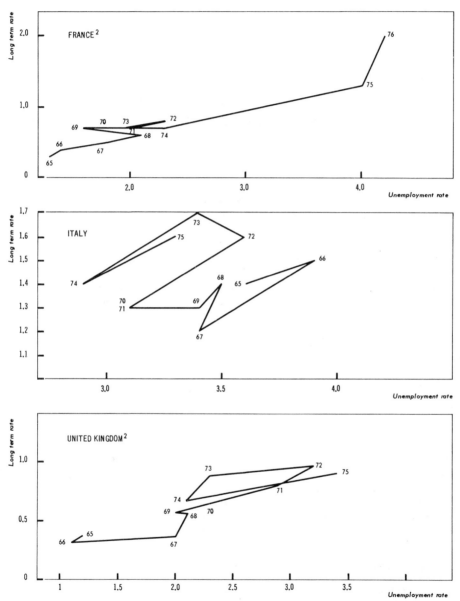

1. USA long term unemployment rate : unemployed over 26 weeks.
2. March of every year.
3. UK long term unemployment rate : unemployed over 27 weeks, Great Btitain only.

Sources : National sources.

117

ESTIMATES OF THE CHANGING COMPOSITION OF UNEMPLOYMENT

As described in the main text of this Report, there is considerable uncertainty concerning the factors underlying the increase in unemployment in recent years. At the same time, however, in framing policies to reduce unemployment, it is important to try to establish how far present unemployment can be explained by a cyclical shortage of aggregate demand. This will indicate the scope for a recovery in aggregate demand and output to bring about a reduction in unemployment without aggravating inflationary pressure, while any further reduction will depend upon the other complementary policies described in this Report.

The quantitative estimates of the changing structure of unemployment described in this Annex are based on a three-way classification of unemployment into cyclical unemployment, capital-shortage unemployment and frictional unemployment. Cyclical unemployment is defined as that unemployment associated directly with any "short-fall" in aggregate demand. Typically, cyclical unemployment will be matched by a corresponding short-fall in the rate of capital utilisation. Capital-shortage unemployment is that unemployment resulting from any capacity constraints which, with given relative factor prices or limitations on factor substitution, could only be remedied by more rapid expansion of the capital stock[1]. In effect, therefore, both cyclical and capital-shortage unemployment can be reduced by macro-economic demand management policies, though the latter category may require a longer period of adjustment possibly accompanied by supporting policies to adjust relative factor prices. The estimate for frictional unemployment represents the balance of unemployment, reflecting such factors as normal labour turnover or slow

---

1. At a given set of factor prices it is assumed that the level of employment is determined, *inter alia,* by the capital stock. The stock may then be insufficient to ensure full employment if:
   - there has been under-investment in the past because of lack of demand or profitability;
   - higher real wages or other basic input prices (e.g. energy) have rendered old equipment uneconomic, leading to more rapid scrapping of the existing capital stock and/or new investment in labour-saving equipment;
   - rapid increase in the aggregate supply of labour has not been compensated by a sufficient downward adjustment in real wages relative to earlier trends.

adjustment to various mismatches in the labour market, including some features often described as "structural", such as the types of skills available and demanded, the regional distribution of employment opportunities, and so on. Frictional unemployment will also reflect any supply-side influences affecting people's willingness to work at the going wage rate, such as might result from changes in the level or availability of unemployment compensation.

Using this classification of unemployment, the process of non-inflationary recovery in the labour market can be thought of as having three aspects or phases. In the first, the critical issue will be the rate at which aggregate demand (globally and/or selectively) can be expanded and unemployment absorbed as the slack is taken up. Even during the first phase, however, it will be important that the conditions are created for further progress in subsequent phases. In particular, the pattern of demand should be such that investment expands capacity sufficiently early so as to avoid capacity shortages and "uncomfortably high" operating rates in the second phase, during which unemployment will be reduced in line with expanding capacity. In the third phase, traditional manpower-adjustment policies which reduce basic structural impediments to adjustment are especially important, as the main constraint to further expansion then stems directly from labour market rigidities and inflationary pressures reflecting tightness in particular segments of labour markets.

Although it is helpful in framing policies to distinguish these three aspects and time phases of labour market adjustment in order to better focus the relevant policy instruments, care should of course be taken with their interpretation. In the first place, the estimates of the three types of unemployment necessarily involve a considerable element of judgment concerning the exact magnitude of the different factors affecting the labour market, so that at best the estimates can only serve as guide to policy action. Secondly, to an important degree, the different types of unemployment are interdependent. Thus, as is described in the main text above, the amount of frictional unemployment can be expected to increase in a cyclical down-turn as labour market rigidities increase in response to greater job insecurity. Similarly, the risk of future capital-shortage unemployment will also be increased in a prolonged recession as the incentive to invest declines. The complementary nature of manpower and demand management policies must therefore not be overlooked. Demand management policies providing for a soundly-based economic recovery can help in reducing labour market rigidities and in encouraging the investment necessary to avoid future bottlenecks. While in the short-run manpower policies are frequently directed to sharing and reducing the burden of unemployment in what is seen as necessarily a protracted recovery process, in the longer-run they have the potential to improve the flexibility of demand management policies by facilitating labour market adjustment processes.

If a properly integrated and phased approach to reducing unemployment is adopted, based on the recognition of these three types of unemployment, then it should be possible to achieve a new "full-employment" equilibrium without any inflationary pressures from the labour market. In the short run, therefore, the "natural" or "full-employment" rate of unemployment, consistent with no acceleration in inflation, can be regarded as actual unemployment less cyclical unemployment. But in the longer run if capacity is expanded so as to avoid any capacity bottlenecks, then the full-employment rate of unemployment could be reduced to the level of frictional unemployment, which itself might be lowered in response to policies and as labour-market adjustment mechanisms improve.

METHODOLOGICAL APPROACH

The present analysis and estimates of unemployment are based on a separate examination of labour demand on the one hand and labour supply on the other. Unemployment is then determined as the difference between labour demand and supply. Despite the operational difficulties of obtaining accurate results with this approach, it is preferred for conceptual reasons to the alternative of analysing directly the relationship between unemployment and the pressure of aggregate demand. The relationship between these two variables has varied considerably, and the changes can only be comprehended following a separate analysis of the various factors other than aggregate demand which influence labour demand and supply. Furthermore, one of the benefits of this approach is that it shows how the increase in employment through the recovery period can proceed quite independently from any reduction in unemployment. In fact, it would seem that not only is there not a one-for-one relationship between employment and unemployment, but the relation between the two changes over time so that during the cycle the number of jobs that have to be created in order to reduce unemployment by one unit will vary considerably.

The actual analysis of labour supply and demand was initially based on a sample model estimated for the years from 1960 to 1973. The coefficients obtained were then used to simulate the most recent period from 1974 to 1976. The specification of the equations, along with the actual regression results obtained, are shown in Tables 1 and 2. Labour demand was assumed to be derived from a neo-classical production function which relates the desired demand for labour to the available capital stock and its rate of utilisation, a substitution effect reflecting the relative costs of labour and capital[2], and technological progress (that is to say time)[3]. The adjustment of effective to desired employment is assumed to occur only after some lag, and the degree of adjustment is also affected by whether policy is assumed to be contractionary or expansionary (as described by the movement in the real interest rate). Where there was a very strong trend in the self-employed, their labour demand was separately estimated as this had the advantage of removing the influence of falling employment in agriculture which in many cases reflected a response to social changes rather than economic demand. The labour-supply function used represents only a very rudimentary separation of cyclical and trend movements in the overall participation rate and population changes. It could certainly be improved with greater disaggregation and more work analysing trends in participation rates.

Estimates of the frictional component of unemployment are based on a number of exogenous sources and studies. They reflect estimates of the impact on unemployment of:

    i) the changing age and sex structure of the work force;

---

2. The relative cost of labour and capital was measured as the ratio between the compensation per employee and the user cost of capital. The latter was defined as the product of the short-term interest rate and the deflator of capital goods. The effect of fiscal changes was not taken into account, and neither was the possibility of capital gains.

3. A more appropriate macro-economic specification of the equation might be obtained by substituting output for capital as an explanatory variable, and in some cases this permits the estimation of an equation for employment demand with better statistical properties. This specification however assumes that capital is variable and output is fixed and strictly excludes the possibility of structural unemployment. Therefore, in order to maintain a uniform conceptual framework allowing the possibility of structural unemployment, the results obtained by specifying the demand for labour functions as a function of the available capital stock have almost always been retained.

Table 1. **Demand for labour equation**

	C	LCK	LRP	TI	LGDP	R²	DW	SE
Canada (Total employment)	-2.13 (1.46)	.72 (11.83)	-.017 (1.80)	-.19 (4.14)		.997	2.02	.008
United States (Total employment)	5.03 (1.30)	.501 (3.44)	-.041 (1.86)	-.048 (.686)		.986	0.870	.011
Japan (Dependent employment)	14.11 (21.29)	.077 (3.35)	-.048 (.405)	.278 (9.10)		.997	1.64	.008
Germany (Dependent employment)	6.77 (2.72)	.393 (4.09)	-.011 (.905)	-.260 (3.24)		.830	1.22	.009
France (Dependent employment)	11.43 (8.05)	.176 (3.39)	-.012 (7.90)	.10 (7.90)		.994	1.15	.007
Italy (Dependent employment)	1.46 (0.35)	.490 (0.73)	-.030 (2.51)	-.24 (2.06)		.854	1.22	.018
United Kingdom (Total employment)	16.95 (323.1)		-.038 (2.99)		.011 (3.65)	.840	0.77	.010
Sweden	.231 (.063)	.584 (3.89)		-.208 2.24		.973	1.35	.010

Figures in brackets are t statistics.
The demand for labour was determined as:
$$LEE^* = C_1 + \alpha_1 LCK + \beta_1 LRP + \gamma_1 TI \text{ and}$$
$$LEE = C_2 + \alpha_2 LR + \beta_2 LEE^* + \gamma_2 LEE^* \qquad (-1) \qquad (-2)$$

where
EE* = desired employment
EE = actual employment
CK = capital stock adjusted by utilisation rate
RP = factor price ratio
R = real interest rate (a proxy for policy changes and affecting adjusting speeds)
TI = time
GDP = real output.
The prefix "L" for each variable indicates that logarithms have been taken.

Table 2. Participation rates equation

	C	TI	LGDP	LGAP	LGAP (−1)	R²	DW	SE
Canada	−7.75 (6.68)	−.114 (3.38)	.302 (6.08)			.987	1.92	.003
United States	.57 (44.4)	.053 (10.6)			−.18 (3.34)	.926	1.80	.004
Japan	−3.60 (3.30)	−.180 (3.68)	.118 (3.07)			.799	1.10	.005
Germany	−.25 (31.8)	−.048 (15.48)		.18 (3.75)		.963	1.64	.002
France	−3.66 (5.52)	−.072 (4.04)	.125 (4.83)			.830	2.05	.002
Italy	−5.08 (3.57)	−.24 (3.10)	.162 (3.43)			.983	2.16	.005
United Kingdom	−.37 (44.8)	.012 (3.60)		.15 (1.61)		.545	1.40	.004
Sweden	−.49 (10.9)	.073 (4.48)		.09 (.030)		.815	0.88	.008

Figures in brackets are t statistics.
The supply of labour was determined as:
LBF = PR × POP and
LPR = $C_3 + \alpha_3$ LTI + β_3 LGAP.
where LBF = labour force
  PR = participation rate
  POP = population of working age (14-64)
  GAP = GDP gap
  TI = time.
The prefix "L" for each variable (except LBF) indicates that logarithms have been taken.

ii) abnormal increases in youth unemployment possibly associated with changes to wage structures;

iii) increasing labour turnover and changing hoarding practices;

iv) improved access to unemployment compensation and benefits; and

v) other government measures affecting job mobility, including internal and external migration.

A first estimate of the cyclical component of unemployment was derived by taking the difference between the model estimates of actual unemployment and the estimates when the capacity utilisation and demand pressure variables in the model were set at their full employment values. An independent estimate of structural unemployment was similarly derived by taking the difference between the model estimate of actual unemployment and another estimate of unemployment obtained from the model, but where relative factor prices and the capital stock were set at levels consistent with maintaining the long run equilibrium growth of labour productivity[4].

If the regression equations describing labour demand and supply from 1960 to 1973 were an accurate representation of present labour market behaviour, and if the various independent variables were correctly estimated, then the independent estimates of frictional, cyclical and structural unemployment would add to the total of observed unemployment. As might be expected, however, there were discrepancies between the independent estimates of unemployment and the observed total. A more detailed analysis of labour demand and supply, and the various sources of simulation error, then helped in resolving these discrepancies. One major advantage of the procedure adopted, however, is that total recorded unemployment effectively acted as a control on the estimation, and in the end any remaining discrepancy between the model estimates and that total could be attributed judgementally to the three unemployment components.

The first major source of error in the independent model estimates seemed to be changed labour-hoarding behaviour by businesses. Labour hoarding is a normal response by business to a cyclical downturn which it expects to be quickly reversed, and reflects the cost and uncertainty of firing people and then subsequently rehiring them as demand and output recover. It can, however, be expected that the incentive to hoard will weaken if business confidence falls during a prolonged recession, and that with time, unless labour demand recovers, effective employment will be reduced. In the present study, where the model estimates of employment differed from observed employment, this was usually assumed to indicate a change in labour hoarding practices. For the most part, independent analysis of labour hoarding suggested that a variety of government measures have softened the impact of the recession on cyclical unemployment and the original model estimate of cyclical unemployment was therefore adjusted accordingly.

The other major source of error was in the simulation of the labour supply. The analysis of labour supply suggested that the equations employed in the model tended to underpredict the present labour supply and there are a number of possible reasons for this. Reference has already been made to the possible impact of increases in unemployment compensation on labour supply, and, where this was thought to have led to a permanent increase in the level of unemployment associated with a given demand pressure, the estimate of frictional unemployment was accordingly increased. For the

---

4. Obviously, fixing the factor-price ratio and the associated level of the capital stock involve and important degree of rather arbitrary guess-work.

balance of any under-prediction of labour supply, it was necessary to determine whether this represented a cyclical response different from the average response in previous recessions, or whether there had been a long-term upward shift in the supply of labour. A different cyclical response would reflect the effect of improved unemployment benefits and the work of employment agencies, encouraging groups such as married women to remain in the labour force when they become unemployed, whereas previously they had tended to leave. On the other hand, another factor which may have emerged in a prolonged and deep recession is the "additional" worker. Because of the loss of family income, the recession may have induced members of the family unit who were not previously in the labour force to seek employment in order to compensate for the loss of income from the principal "bread-winner"[5]. Where it was thought that there have been either fewer discouraged workers, or more additional workers, an addition was made to the estimate of cyclical unemployment. Otherwise there was a tendency to treat the remaining "unexplained" increase in the labour supply as a permanent increase and thus as an increase in the amount of structural unemployment until either the capital stock is increased or relative factor prices adjust.

INDIVIDUAL COUNTRY EXPERIENCE

Although, as already noted, there was a general tendency to under-predict the labour supply from 1974 to 1976, the degree of under-prediction varied considerably across countries. At one end of the spectrum were Sweden and the United Kingdom where the recent increase in supply appears especially abnormal. During the 1960's and the beginning of the 1970's in Sweden, for example, the average participation rates oscillated around 0.74, showing a very small increasing trend. In 1974, however, the Swedish average participation rate rose to 0.77 and in 1975 it almost reached 0.79. This corresponds to an increase in the labour supply of almost 7 per cent in two years, an increase which has hardly any precedent in the OECD area. The United Kingdom's experience was very similar, with the average participation rate oscillating around 0.70 during the 1960's and beginning of the 1970's, and then jumping to 0.72 and 0.725 in 1974 and 1975 respectively. If the small trend increase in average labour force participation had been maintained, along with a normal response to the pressure of demand, then in 1976 it is estimated that there would have been about 400,000 fewer workers in the British labour force.

The reasons for this "unexpected" increase in the participation rates in Sweden and the United Kingdom may, however, have differed. In both countries measures have been taken during the recession to improve their systems of unemployment compensation, but mainly by way of more generous allowances; there has been little change in the eligibility conditions. On this basis it seems unlikely that the changes in unemployment compensation have led to very much of the observed increase in the labour supply. Instead in Sweden the most important influence on the labour supply may have been via the impact of the measures taken to maintain employment during the recession.

5. As noted below, such a draw from the non-labour force population into the labour force is also very often a feature of direct employment programmes run by government agencies.

Table 3. Hoarding[1] as a percentage of labour force

	United States	Canada	Japan	Germany	France	Italy	United Kingdom
1974	1.6	1.3	3.6	0.5	0.8	1.0	2.5
1975	2.2	2.9	4.4	3.0	1.4	3.5	3.3
1976	1.4	1.8	2.7	0.8	1.0	1.6	3.5
Productivity (Growth rates)							
1964-73	2.1	2.3	8.8	4.7	4.9	5.3	2.9
1973-74	-3.6	-1.4	-0.7	2.5	3.2	1.2	-0.5
1974-75	-0.5	-0.8	2.6	0.1	1.2	-4.0	-1.2
1975-76	2.8	2.5	5.4	6.7	5.1	4.9	2.3

1. Number of full-time equivalent employees who could be laid off without affecting output. The results are not necessarily comparable between countries.

Table 4. Components of unemployment

	Actual unemployment rate[1]	Cyclical unemployment	Unemployment at full capacity of existing capital stock	Frictional unemployment	Capital-shortage unemployment
UNITED STATES					
1974	5.5	0.6	4.9	4.9	0.0
1975	8.4	3.3	5.1	4.9	0.2
1976	7.6	2.1	5.5	4.9	0.6
CANADA					
1974	5.3	0.1	5.2	5.2	0.0
1975	6.9	1.1	5.8	5.6	0.2
1976	7.1	0.6	6.5	6.0	0.5
JAPAN					
1974	1.4	0.3	1.1	1.1	0.0
1975	1.9	0.7	1.2	1.1	0.1
1976	2.0	0.7	1.3	1.1	0.2
FRANCE					
1974	2.8	0.3	2.5	2.4	0.1
1975	4.1	1.3	2.8	2.4	0.4
1976	4.5	1.1	3.4	2.5	0.9
UNITED KINGDOM					
1974	2.2	0.1	2.1	2.0	0.1
1975	3.4	0.7	2.7	2.2	0.5
1976	5.0	1.7	3.3	2.4	0.9
SWEDEN					
1974	2.0	0.3	. .	1.6	0.1
1975	1.6	0.0	. .	1.6	0.0
1976	1.6	0.0	. .	1.6	0.0
GERMANY					
1974	2.2	0.4	1.8	1.5	0.3
1975	4.2	1.2	3.0	2.2	0.8
1976	4.1	0.6	3.5	2.5	1.0
ITALY					
1974	5.9	0.1	5.8	5.0	0.8
1975	6.7	0.3	6.4	5.0	1.4
1976	7.2	0.4	6.8	5.0	1.8
NETHERLANDS					
1974	3.0	0.5	2.5	1.6	0.9
1975	4.3	1.4	2.9	1.8	1.1
1976	4.7	1.2	3.5	2.0	1.5

1. *Source:* OECD, *Labour Force Statistics.* The unemployment rate is here defined as the ratio of unemployed to civilian Labour Force. The actual unemployment rate is the sum of cyclical unemployment and unemployment at full capacity of the existing capital stock. The latter is the sum of frictional and capital shortage unemployment.

These may have encouraged many people mainly on the fringe of the labour force (for example, women) to offer themselves for employment. Where measures to sustain employment take the form of direct job creation, and especially if those jobs are in the service sector, then it is likely that many of the jobs will be taken by people who otherwise would not have maintained their labour force participation or even by people who were not previously in the labour force[6]. Attempts along these lines at job creation were not so important in the United Kingdom before 1976 and thus this type of effect seems unlikely to account for the increase in the labour supply in that country. Instead a tentative but unproven hypothesis might be that it is the slow growth of real incomes which induced families to increase their labour supply.

In North America there was also a tendency to under-predict the labour supply, but to a lesser extent than in Sweden or the United Kingdom. In Canada an important cause of the apparent increase in labour supply seems to have been the response to the more generous unemployment system introduced by the reform of 1971. But as in Sweden, the Local Initiative Program in Canada may also have encouraged people to remain in the labour force or to join the labour force during the recession. Where the separate estimates of this effect are included, they largely account for the under-prediction in the labour supply equation used here. By contrast, in the United States the "Emergency Unemployment Compensation Act" is unlikely to have accounted for all of the extra increase in labour supply as there was some under-prediction in 1974 and the Act only came into operation at the beginning of 1975. What seems to have been happening is that the discouraged worker phenomenon has been less important in this recession.

In Italy there has been a long-term trend towards lower labour-force participation, possibly reflecting a structural increase in the number of discouraged workers who believe that they have little chance of ever obtaining regular employment, and also the development of a parallel labour market which partly represented an attempt to avoid various forms of taxation. In the last few years, however, the declining trend in workforce participation has been reversed, and if the government moves successfully to control the "black" labour market then it is likely that, in future, unemployment will play the adjustment role during a period of weak labour demand that participation rates have played so far. In France, Germany and Japan the labour supply functions predicted very closely the recorded labour supply and in Germany they even over-predicted. In that country it would seem that participation rates have fallen more rapidly than might have been expected, possibly because the return migration has affected people with a high rate of labour force participation. Another possible cause of over-prediction is the change in the age structure of the labour force and the larger share in it of young people with lower participation rates.

On the side of the demand for labour, it would seem that the movement in labour hoarding is generally consistent with the change in labour productivity. Generally labour hoarding is shown as increasing when the change in productivity is less than its long run trend increase and vice versa (see Table 1). No exact comparisons between the rate of labour hoarding and productivity increase can be made however, because the change in productivity

6. In France independent studies suggest that six jobs in the public sector need to be created to reduce unemployment by one, largely because many of the jobs will be taken up by people not presently in the labour force. See Christian Sautter and Jean-Michel Charpin "L'Emploi à Moyen Terme - Politique de Réduction du Chômage", Paper presented to Conference of European Planners, Jerusalem, 1977.

reflects a number of factors apart from labour hoarding. In particular, in those countries where an important element of aggregate productivity increase reflects the movement of labour from less productive to more productive industries, the deceleration of aggregate productivity during the recession may largely reflect a slower rate of structural change rather than any marked increase in labour hoarding by individual enterprises. Of the countries shown, it is thought that the relationship between the pace of structural adjustment and aggregate productivity change may be especially important in France, Italy and Japan, although in Japan's case there has also been a bigger decline in trend productivity growth than elsewhere.

A particular feature of hoarding in the recent recession was that, on the whole, in most countries it seems to have been higher than would have been expected from previous experience. To some extent this may reflect the success of government measures aimed at sustaining employment by way of financial help to industries and in some cases by direct job creation. It may also reflect the changes in social legislation which have made the retrenchment of labour much more costly and difficult. However, in this latter case at least, it might be expected that with time businesses will be able to reduce their employment levels to something more closely approximating that desired, as employment is generally reduced by retirements and people leaving not being replaced. Indeed, there is a possibility that this may already have been occurring. It may be noted, for example, that in France and Germany employment *fell* in 1976 while at the same time there was a fairly strong recovery in output. In Canada and Japan, which are estimated to have a high degree of hoarding, the growth of employment in 1976 was almost 1 percentage point lower than the long-term trend, despite the fact that output growth was approximately in line with potential growth, or even above it in the case of Canada. In the United Kingdom, employment has been falling recently and there may have been further increase in labour hoarding, or even some reduction in the private sector if allowance is made for the impact of the Government's direct employment-creating programmes. Finally, and in contrast with experience elsewhere, in the United States, the degree of labour hoarding was never particularly high, and so a faster-than-trend growth in output in 1976 was more or less matched by a faster-than-trend growth in employment.

A general problem with the estimates of labour hoarding is that they may be biased by errors in the estimates of labour demand. If cyclical unemployment has been under-estimated or if there has been more capital deepening than allowed for in the labour demand equations, then the desired level of employment would be over-estimated, and as a consequence the present level of labour hoarding would be under-estimated. This could be part of the explanation for what seems to be a somewhat lower *level* of labour hoarding in France and Germany than in the other countries shown. It may also reflect the problem of labour hoarding in Sweden and the Netherlands for which separate estimates of labour hoarding are not shown. In Sweden's case the best estimates of frictional unemployment account for all the recorded unemployment. As it is difficult to believe that there has been no cyclical or structural unemployment during the last few years, the most probable explanation would seem to be that these other two sources of unemployment have been fully offset by labour hoarding.

In the Netherlands, it is thought that capital-labour substitution may have proceeded even further than elsewhere and certainly the performance of the labour demand equation derived for that country was exceptionally poor. It would seem that a major change in the demand for labour in the Netherlands occurred about the beginning of the 1970's and that employment has been nearly flat from then onwards. This could be because of changes in the composition of output towards more capital-intensive production or because of a shift in relative factor prices. In the latter case the labour-demand equation used should have captured some of the impact, but it is understood that the Netherlands authorities have obtained rather better results using a vintage model of the capital stock[7].

Finally, in considering capital-labour substitution, it might also be noted that the previous tendency for the cost of labour to increase relative to the cost of capital seems to have been reversed in a number of countries in the last two or three years. So far, however, this has not led to the increase in employment which might have been expected from the labour demand equations. This may be because employers are reducing their degree of labour hoarding or because there are longer lags in the adjustment of employment to changes in relative factor prices than to other factors affecting the demand for labour. It may also be, however, that the joint increase of both the user cost of capital and employees' remuneration has squeezed profits thus lowering the propensity to invest and to hire new workers. At any event, it does seem to suggest that a downward adjustment in the relative cost of labour may not help employment demand very much when there is already a large degree of slack for other reasons.

Turning to consider the changes in the composition of unemployment in the different countries examined, it is perhaps most interesting to note that in all countries examined frictional unemployment is estimated to account for roughly half or more of recorded unemployment. Furthermore, there has been some tendency for the level of frictional unemployment to increase in recent years; a tendency which may have been most marked in Germany, but which was also significant in Canada, the Netherlands and the United Kingdom. Of the various factors which have been cited as causes of frictional unemployment, and which might have been expected to increase during the last few years of recession, perhaps the most important for each of these countries is the changing significance of migration. In Germany, in particular, much migration has been of a short-run nature. As a result, the German labour market typically experienced large inflows and outflows of migrant labour and search time and other rigidities in the labour market were greatly reduced by the possibility of hiring from abroad the specific types of manpower needed. Now it may be questioned whether the new German entrants to the labour force will be prepared to undertake all those jobs previously performed by immigrants, and whether in the absence of renewed immigration this will not therefore tend to generate a permanently higher rate of frictional unemployment.

Apart from the unemployment attributed to frictional causes, it is generally estimated that cyclical unemployment was predominant at the trough of the recession in 1975. But already by 1976, future capital-shortage was emerging as more important than cyclical unemployment, reflecting the sluggishness of investment during the last few years. In most countries, however, the cyclical component of unemployment is estimated to be still very large in 1976. With some exceptions, this suggests that there is still substantial scope for expanding

7. H. den Hortog and H.S. Tjan: *Investments, wages, prices and demand for labour*, Reprint Series No. 156, Central Planning Bureau, The Hague; C.A. van der Beld, "Employment Growth in the collective sector versus the Enterprise sector", in: *Structural Determinants of Employment and Unemployment*, Vol. II, OECD, forthcoming.

demand without hitting any bottlenecks caused by insufficient capital stock.

The countries where the cyclical component is estimated to be the largest are the United States, the United Kingdom, and to a lesser degree France and the Netherlands. In the United States structural unemployment is not estimated to be very much of a problem, although it may begin to be a problem if recent trends continue. By contrast in the Netherlands and Germany capital-shortage unemployment is shown as being rather large compared to cyclical, but the estimated magnitude seems to be broadly consistent with present rates of *capital* utilisation, the availability of capital relative to the labour supply and movements in relative factor prices over the last ten years or so.

In one sense, the figure shown for Italy definitely under-estimates capital-shortage unemployment because in that country participation rates are unusually low compared to other industrialised countries. It is possible, therefore, that an even greater increase in capital accumulation would be required in that country than elsewhere in order to reduce unemployment to acceptable levels.

OECD SALES AGENTS
DÉPOSITAIRES DES PUBLICATIONS DE L'OCDE

ARGENTINA — ARGENTINE
Carlos Hirsch S.R.L., Florida 165,
BUENOS-AIRES, ☎ 33-1787-2391 Y 30-7122

AUSTRALIA — AUSTRALIE
International B.C.N. Library Suppliers Pty Ltd.,
161 Sturt St., South MELBOURNE, Vic. 3205. ☎ 699-6388
P.O.Box 202, COLLAROY, NSW 2097 ☎ 982 4515

AUSTRIA — AUTRICHE
Gerold and Co., Graben 31, WIEN 1. ☎ 52.22.35

BELGIUM — BELGIQUE
Librairie des Sciences,
Coudenberg 76-78, B 1000 BRUXELLES 1. ☎ 512-05-60

BRAZIL — BRÉSIL
Mestre Jou S.A., Rua Guaipá 518,
Caixa Postal 24090, 05089 SAO PAULO 10. ☎ 261-1920
Rua Senador Dantas 19 s/205-6, RIO DE JANEIKO GB.
☎ 232-07. 32

CANADA
Renouf Publishing Company Limited,
2182 St. Catherine Street West,
MONTREAL, Quebec H3H 1M7 ☎ (514) 937-3519

DENMARK — DANEMARK
Munksgaards Boghandel,
Nørregade 6, 1165 KØBENHAVN K. ☎ (01) 12 69 70

FINLAND — FINLANDE
Akateeminen Kirjakauppa
Keskuskatu 1, 00100 HELSINKI 10. ☎ 625.901

FRANCE
Bureau des Publications de l'OCDE,
2 rue André-Pascal, 75775 PARIS CEDEX 16.
☎ 524.81.67
Principal correspondant :
13602 AIX-EN-PROVENCE : Librairie de l'Université.
☎ 26.18.08

GERMANY — ALLEMAGNE
Verlag Weltarchiv G.m.b.H.
D 2000 HAMBURG 36, Neuer Jungfernstieg 21.
☎ 040-35-62-500

GREECE — GRÈCE
Librairie Kauffmann, 28 rue du Stade,
ATHÈNES 132. ☎ 322.21.60

HONG-KONG
Government Information Services,
Sales and Publications Office, Beaconsfield House, 1st floor,
Queen's Road, Central. ☎ H-233191

ICELAND — ISLANDE
Snaebjörn Jónsson and Co., h.f.,
Hafnarstraeti 4 and 9, P.O.B. 1131, REYKJAVIC.
☎ 13133/14281/11936

INDIA — INDE
Oxford Book and Stationery Co.:
NEW DELHI, Scindia House. ☎ 45896
CALCUTTA, 17 Park Street. ☎ 240832

IRELAND - IRLANDE
Eason and Son, 40 Lower O'Connell Street,
P.O.B. 42, DUBLIN 1. ☎ 74 39 35

ISRAËL
Emanuel Brown: 35 Allenby Road, TEL AVIV. ☎ 51049/54082
also at:
9, Shlomzion Hamalka Street, JERUSALEM. ☎ 234807
48 Nahlath Benjamin Street, TEL AVIV. ☎ 53276

ITALY — ITALIE
Libreria Commissionaria Sansoni:
Via Lamarmora 45, 50121 FIRENZE. ☎ 579751
Via Bartolini 29, 20155 MILANO. ☎ 365083
Sous-dépositaires :
Editrice e Libreria Herder,
Piazza Montecitorio 120, 00 186 ROMA. ☎ 674628
Libreria Hoepli, Via Hoepli 5, 20121 MILANO. ☎ 865446
Libreria Lattes, Via Garibaldi 3, 10122 TORINO. ☎ 519274
La diffusione delle edizioni OCDE è inoltre assicurata dalle migliori

JAPAN — JAPON
OECD Publications Centre,
Akasaka Park Building, 2-3-4 Akasaka, Minato-ku,
TOKYO 107. ☎ 586-2016

KOREA - CORÉE
Pan Korea Book Corporation,
P.O.Box n° 101 Kwangwhamun, SÉOUL. ☎ 72-7369

LEBANON — LIBAN
Documenta Scientifica/Redico,
Edison Building, Bliss Street, P.O.Box 5641, BEIRUT.
☎ 354429—344425

THE NETHERLANDS — PAYS-BAS
Staatsuitgeverij
Chr. Plantijnstraat
'S-GRAVENHAGE. ☎ 070-814511
Voor bestellingen: ☎ 070-624551

NEW ZEALAND - NOUVELLE-ZÉLANDE
The Publications Manager,
Government Printing Office,
WELLINGTON: Mulgrave Street (Private Bag),
World Trade Centre, Cubacade, Cuba Street,
Rutherford House, Lambton Quay, ☎ 737-320
AUCKLAND: Rutland Street (P.O.Box 5344), ☎ 32.919
CHRISTCHURCH: 130 Oxford Tce (Private Bag), ☎ 50.331
HAMILTON: Barton Street (P.O.Box 857), ☎ 80.103
DUNEDIN: T & G Building, Princes Street (P.O.Box 1104),
☎ 78.294

NORWAY — NORVÈGE
Johan Grundt Tanums Bokhandel,
Karl Johansgate 41/43, OSLO 1. ☎ 02-332980

PAKISTAN
Mirza Book Agency, 65 Shahrah Quaid-E-Azam, LAHORE 3.
☎ 66839

PHILIPPINES
R.M. Garcia Publishing House, 903 Quezon Blvd. Ext.,
QUEZON CITY, P.O.Box 1860 — MANILA. ☎ 99.98.47

PORTUGAL
Livraria Portugal, Rua do Carmo 70-74, LISBOA 2. ☎ 360582/3

SPAIN — ESPAGNE
Mundi-Prensa Libros, S.A.
Castelló 37, Apartado 1223, MADRID-1. ☎ 275.46.55
Libreria Bastinos, Pelayo, 52, BARCELONA 1. ☎ 222.06.00

SWEDEN — SUÈDE
AB CE FRITZES KUNGL HOVBOKHANDEL,
Box 16 356, S 103 27 STH, Regeringsgatan 12,
DS STOCKHOLM. ☎ 08/23 89 00

SWITZERLAND — SUISSE
Librairie Payot, 6 rue Grenus, 1211 GENÈVE 11. ☎ 022-31.89.50

TAIWAN — FORMOSE
National Book Company,
84-5 Sing Sung Rd., Sec. 3, TAIPEI 107. ☎ 321.0698

TURKEY — TURQUIE
Librairie Hachette,
469 Istiklal Caddesi, Beyoglu, ISTANBUL. ☎ 44.94.70
et 14 E Ziya Gökalp Caddesi, ANKARA. ☎ 12.10.80

UNITED KINGDOM — ROYAUME-UNI
H.M. Stationery Office, P.O.B. 569,
LONDON SEI 9 NH. ☎ 01-928-6977, Ext.410
or
49 High Holborn, LONDON WC1V 6 HB (personal callers)
Branches at: EDINBURGH, BIRMINGHAM, BRISTOL,
MANCHESTER, CARDIFF, BELFAST.

UNITED STATES OF AMERICA
OECD Publications Center, Suite 1207, 1750 Pennsylvania Ave.,
N.W. WASHINGTON, D.C.20006. ☎ (202)298-8755

VENEZUELA
Libreria del Este, Avda. F. Miranda 52, Edificio Galipán,
CARACAS 106. ☎ 32 23 01/33 26 04/33 24 73

YUGOSLAVIA — YOUGOSLAVIE
Jugoslovenska Knjiga, Terazije 27, P.O.B. 36, BEOGRAD.
☎ 621-992

Les commandes provenant de pays où l'OCDE n'a pas encore désigné de dépositaire peuvent être adressées à :
OCDE, Bureau des Publications, 2 rue André-Pascal, 75775 PARIS CEDEX 16.
Orders and inquiries from countries where sales agents have not yet been appointed may be sent to:
OECD, Publications Office, 2 rue André-Pascal, 75775 PARIS CEDEX 16.

OECD PUBLICATIONS, 2, rue André-Pascal, 75775 Paris Cedex 16 - No. 40.743 1978
PRINTED IN FRANCE